ROUTLEDGE LIBRARY EDITIONS:
MARRIAGE

I0127425

Volume 15

MARRIAGE
UNDER STRESS

MARRIAGE UNDER STRESS

A Comparative Study of Marriage Conciliation

GERALD SANCTUARY

Routledge
Taylor & Francis Group

LONDON AND NEW YORK

First published in 1968 by George Allen & Unwin Ltd

This edition first published in 2023
by Routledge
4 Park Square, Milton Park, Abingdon, Oxon OX14 4RN

and by Routledge
605 Third Avenue, New York, NY 10158

Routledge is an imprint of the Taylor & Francis Group, an informa business

British Library Cataloguing in Publication Data
A catalogue record for this book is available from the British Library

ISBN: 978-1-032-46071-0 (Set)
ISBN: 978-1-032-46782-5 (Volume 15) (hbk)
ISBN: 978-1-032-46786-3 (Volume 15) (pbk)
ISBN: 978-1-003-38327-7 (Volume 15) (ebk)

DOI: 10.4324/9781003383277

Publisher's Note
The publisher has gone to great lengths to ensure the quality of this reprint but points out that some imperfections in the original copies may be apparent.

Disclaimer
The publisher has made every effort to trace copyright holders and would welcome correspondence from those they have been unable to trace.

MARRIAGE UNDER STRESS

A Comparative Study of Marriage Conciliation

by

GERALD SANCTUARY

London

GEORGE ALLEN AND UNWIN LTD

RUSKIN HOUSE   MUSEUM STREET

PRINTED IN GREAT BRITAIN
in 11 on 12 point Juliana type
BY THE BLACKFRIARS PRESS LTD
LEICESTER

CONTENTS

INTRODUCTION

Organized attempts to provide marriage conciliation services are one of the new developments of modern society. They have been made necessary by the steadily increasing number of divorces in many parts of the world. Divorces are becoming more and more easy to obtain, and as divorce becomes more common and more socially accepted, so marriages are more easily threatened. Many married couples feel this threat personally, and seek help with their marriage problems from people who hold themselves out as both willing and able to offer specialist and skilled help in strengthening or repairing unstable marital relationships.

In former years it was the function of the grandparent, the uncle or aunt, the neighbour and of the priest to give this kind of help and support. For many people this is still true, but for an increasing number of men and women, living unidentified lives far from their birthplace and from their close relatives, there is no one to turn to. Comparatively few have a deep religious faith to sustain them, and not enough training is being given to young ministers of religion in the methods of pastoral counselling. Unable to talk to a relative or to an old family friend, unwilling to approach neighbours whom they do not fully trust, the unhappy wives and husbands turn frequently to their doctor. Unfortunately the doctor is frequently unable to help because of the existing pressures of his work, or because he feels inadequately trained to give personal counselling.

In most countries the basic unit of society is the family, consisting of the mother, father and children, and sometimes of grandparents and other relatives. Most modern states consider that this family unit is worth preserving. A secure family background enables the growing child to become a useful member of society and to create in his turn a stable and satisfying family unit of his own. Conversely, the insecure or separated family is more likely to produce maladjusted or handicapped children. The great majority of those who have been convicted of serious criminal offences are known to have an unstable family background. It does not of course necessarily follow that when a family is broken its members, especially the children, will fail to

9

adjust to their new situation. Nevertheless, it is generally acknowledged that the risk of such children becoming delinquent is greater than average. Furthermore, it is a common experience for marriage counsellors to be told by their clients that they have themselves come from a broken family background, and children of broken marriages often find difficulty in making satisfactory marital relationships themselves.

Slowly, therefore, marriage counselling and conciliation services have come into being. Some have been established through the efforts of private individuals, some by churches and other organizations, and some by governments. The techniques of marriage counselling have been studied and are being widely taught and practised, and many books exist which give an account of the most effective methods of marriage counselling. Training centres have been set up in different countries and an increasing number of marriage counsellors are now at work.

It would seem that if society is going to permit marriages to be brought to an end in law, it must also provide some opportunity for people who have marital problems to seek help with the intention of avoiding breakdown. Merely to provide the means to end marriage without also providing an opportunity for reconciliation is to invite an ever increasing breakdown of the family unit. It does not very much matter whether the marriage conciliation services are provided by the state, by individuals or by organizations, provided they are competently run and staffed. Marriage counselling is a special skill that can be developed only through training combined with experience, and societies who make no effort to provide it are taking an unnecessary risk.

The purpose of this book is to give some account of the widely differing types of marital conciliation services operating in Britain, and also in some other parts of the world. These services are organized in such a very different way that it seemed appropriate to attempt a comparative study of them. At this early stage of the development of conciliation services my hope is that a comparison could perhaps be useful not only to those who are already engaged in this work, but also to others who may be considering the establishment of new services. It is quite commonplace at the National Headquarters of the National Marriage Guidance Council of Great Britain, where I work, to receive requests for help and for information from many different parts of the world, and the National Council does what it can to respond to these requests. Nevertheless, it is scarcely likely that an organization appropriate in Britain will suit other countries with very different social and cultural backgrounds. My intention in this book therefore, is to give some indication of the wide field of choice of marital conciliation services that now exists.

My own work in this field has been mainly with the National Marriage Guidance Council in Britain and for this reason the first chapters of the book deal with the work of that Council and of the other counselling and conciliation agencies operating in Britain. The first conciliation services to be set up in the world on any scale were in the United States of America, and I have devoted a further two chapters to a short account of developments in that country. The remaining chapters give a brief description of the services operating in Canada, Australia, New Zealand and Scandinavia, and the concluding chapter contains some personal views on the most appropriate methods of associating the work of the marriage counsellor with that of the Courts of Law.

My basic experience in marriage counselling has also been with the National Marriage Guidance Council, but the fact that I have also qualified and practised in the Law for several years has given me an additional interest in the relationship between the Law of Divorce and the process of marital reconciliation. Without the help of countless friends and colleagues in the many different agencies mentioned or described in the following pages, it would have been quite impossible for me to have prepared this book. To them, to my colleagues at the National Marriage Guidance Council and to the people whom I have been privileged to meet in Britain, in Scandinavia and other parts of Europe, and in the United States, I extend my warmest gratitude. But in doing so I take full responsibility for any errors and omissions that there may be in the chapters that follow. It has taken all of three years to prepare this book for publication, and even during that time it has been frequently necessary to amend it and to add new material. The information concerning the National Marriage Guidance Council is accurate and up-to-date at the time of going to print. I am conscious that there may well be neglected areas of the world that fully deserve inclusion in these pages. In addition, in the very new and rapidly developing field of marriage conciliation there is a continuing process of change, alteration and expansion. My most compelling reason for attempting the task at all, and perhaps my best excuse, is that no one else seems to have done so.

Chapter 1

THE MARRIAGE GUIDANCE COUNCIL

The National Marriage Guidance Council consists of more than 120 local Marriage Guidance Councils which between them are using the voluntary services of over 1,400 selected and trained counsellors. Over 18,000 marriages were helped in 1966, and in the same year discussion groups were held with more than 65,000 young people in schools, colleges and youth clubs in all parts of the country. The National Council, which acts as a co-ordinating body to all the local Marriage Guidance Councils, receives a government grant through the Home Office amounting to £42,000 a year, and other income from business, private and charitable sources, and with this money the national organisation is administered and the counsellors selected and trained. The Council also publishes a wide range of books and booklets on all aspects of marriage and family life.

The Marriage Guidance Council was inaugurated in 1938 by a small committee of doctors, clergy and social workers who were concerned about the growing problem of divorce, and the increasing tendency to breakdown in family life. In the previous year Mr (now Sir Alan) Herbert's Matrimonial Causes Act of 1937 had become law, and the first result had been a considerable increase in the number of divorces. The new Act enabled a divorce to be obtained on the grounds of adultery, cruelty, desertion, incurable insanity and certain unnatural offences.

The first Chairman of the Council was the Reverend Herbert Gray. The Secretary was Mrs Marjorie Hume, and among its other members were Dr Lilias Blackett Jeffries and Dr Ethel Dukes, the first two Vice-Chairmen. The new Council's first action was to organize a series of conferences and lectures in London for workers dealing with family problems, and see what could be done to arrest the rising tide of marriage and family breakdown. As soon as the name and objects of the new Council became known, requests for help began to come in from people whose marriages were in difficulty. It was in trying to meet these requests for help that the first attempts at marriage counselling were made. At the initial stage, most of the interviews were given by doctors who were interested in and sympathetic towards the aims of the Council, and who saw clients without charge in their own consulting rooms.

The first counselling centre was opened in London in 1943. Had it not been for the start of the Second World War in 1939, this might have been achieved earlier, but considerable delays had been caused between 1939 and 1942. In the latter part of 1942 the Reverend David Mace, now Professor Mace, then a Methodist minister, became secretary of the Council in succession to Mrs Hume. David Mace was from 1945 to 1949 to share this secretarial work with a probation officer who had helped the Council from the beginning, Mr Reginald Pestell, now the Rt. Hon. Lord Wells-Pestell.

The first clients came to the rooms rented by the Council and were seen by a volunteer secretary. Having heard an outline of the problem, the secretary referred clients to one of the professional men and women, doctors, lawyers, probation officers, psychologists, clergy and social workers who were giving their time to the Council. Clients were not visited in their homes, nor in the home of the professional workers, and this practice has continued to the present day, when clients are always seen in the premises used by the Marriage Guidance Council.

After a time it was found that, by listening to the clients' problems, and without attempting to give them any advice or take any action on their behalf, the secretary was in fact giving a very great deal of help and support. More people were recruited for this part of the Council's work and were termed counsellors, a phrase borrowed from the United States of America, where marriage counselling work had already begun. The counsellors were recognized as being able to perform a separate helping function of their own, but the need for professional support and advice continued, as it has to the present day. Every Marriage Guidance Council in the country now has the help of at least one psychiatric and one legal adviser.

The three rooms that the Marriage Guidance Council rented were at No. 78 Duke Street, Mayfair, and there the marriage counselling work went on side by side with the administration of the growing organisation. Centres began to open in other parts of the country, each set up by local people but operating as a branch of the Council in London. The first local Marriage Guidance Council formed outside London was at Sheffield and others were set up at about the same time, during the latter part of the war, in Cheltenham, Birmingham, Manchester, Liverpool, Bath and Bristol. The work at the London centre continued to be inspired by the Chairman, Dr Herbert Gray, who later wrote:

'As I look back over the twelve years since we first made a start, I am chiefly impressed by the sense of compulsion which gripped us, and would not let us go. I do not think that any of us considered that we were important people ... Certainly the venture did look rather desperate. We had no office, no funds, no precedent to guide us. We just had an inescapable conviction that this thing ought to be done, and that as nobody else was trying, we must needs try.'

Perhaps nobody else was trying because of the obvious difficulty of the task, and even the apparent effrontery of attempting it. Many of the public, and certainly the national press, were sceptical to the point of scorn; but the clients kept coming to the counselling rooms in increasing numbers. One of the most common misconceptions was that the counsellors were a collection of busybodies, prying into other people's lives for their own satisfaction. More serious was the charge that the counsellors, being amateurs and largely untrained, were not competent for the task they had set themselves. In fact, in 1946 the Marriage Guidance Council had already started to develop a system of selection and training for its counsellors. Selection was considered to be vital; many people are impelled to volunteer for counselling work for reasons that make them quite unsuitable. Others are unable to cope with the strains that the work imposes, or are so set in their views about themselves and about other people that they are unable to adapt sufficiently to benefit from training. Realizing this, the Council tried to evolve a method of selection that would produce the right kind of people who could then be trained for the work.

The selection procedure had to establish what kind of people the candidates were, and it was not necessary to concentrate on technical qualifications in order to do this. In many countries, though less in Great Britain than in most, much emphasis is placed on educational attainments. Too often, little attention is given to the personality of candidates or to their basic suitability for the work they are to be trained to do. Training is of course essential to the exercise of any skill, trade or profession, but the use a man makes of his training depends on the kind of person he is. No amount of training will make a good doctor, lawyer, priest or probation officer out of an unsuitable person, and it is the same with the marriage counsellor.

The Council was looking for people with the ability to inspire confidence in others, and with a deep and genuine interest in them. Other necessary qualities were a freedom from prejudice, a liberal and tolerant outlook, and a clear perception of the counsellor's own powers and limitations. Counsellors also needed to have a capacity for reasoned analysis of problems. Perhaps the most important of these qualities was that of self-perception. The only instrument available to a counsellor in helping a client is his own personality, and his capacity to understand himself and his motives is the best means he has of sharpening that instrument.

The first selection conferences, as they were called, lasted two days and were staffed by a psychiatrist and by four selectors who were already working as counsellors for the Marriage Guidance Council. Those who were selected went on to be trained at a series of weekly evening lectures for a period of six months. This training pattern changed considerably as time went by, and it is still changing today. At first, no one was able to say with any certainty what form of training would best equip people to become counsellors, and the training programme was evolved by experience rather than from theory. The methods of selection and training used by the Council have been more fully described by the Council's Training Officer, Mr John Wallis, in his book *Someone to Turn To*.[1]

The Councils that were already operating in various parts of the country were under considerable pressure in the years following the war, when the divorce rate rose to a higher level

[1] Routledge and Kegan Paul, 1961.

than ever before. The government appointed a committee, under the chairmanship of Mr Justice (now Lord Justice) Denning, to report on matrimonial procedures, and in February 1947 this committee issued its report. It stated that 'the most striking civilian development in recent times has been the work done by the Marriage Guidance Council', and went on to make two main recommendations, as follows:

'1. There should be a Marriage Welfare Service to afford help and guidance both in preparation for marriage and in difficulties after marriage. It should be sponsored by the State but should not be a State Institution. It should evolve gradually from the existing services and societies. It should not be combined with judicial procedure for divorce but should function quite separately from it.
'2. It should be regarded as a function of the State to give encouragement and, where appropriate, financial assistance to marriage guidance as a form of social service, particularly by grants in aid of the voluntary societies working in this field.'

Much encouraged by the Denning Committee's Report, the existing Marriage Guidance Councils came together to form a National Council which would co-ordinate the work going on all over the country, ensure equality of standards, and could apply to the government for support. This had become urgently necessary, for the National Marriage Guidance Council, as it was now called, was in considerable financial difficulty. A letter appeared in *The Times* appealing for help, and enough money was given to enable the Council to continue operating for a further short period. The Home Secretary set up a Departmental Committee, under the chairmanship of Sir Sidney Harris, to consider grants for the development of marriage guidance, and this Committee made its report in 1948. It mentioned three bodies who were undertaking marriage counselling work and who were deserving of State support; these were the National Marriage Guidance Council, the Catholic Marriage Advisory Council and the Family Welfare Association. The committee recommended that the selection and training of marriage counsellors should be supervised by the Home Office.

The Family Welfare Association, an organization operating

in and around London, had set up the Family Discussion Bureau, whose work is shortly described in Chapter 4. The Catholic Marriage Advisory Council was set up by and for members of the Roman Catholic Church, and adopted methods of training and selection similar to those of the National Marriage Guidance Council. At an early stage the National Marriage Guidance Council had adopted certain 'Aims and Principles', one of which reads: 'Children are the natural fulfilment of marriage and enrich the relationship between husband and wife; nevertheless scientific contraception, when used according to conscience within marriage, can contribute to the health and happiness of the whole family.' Members of the Roman Catholic Church were not able to accept this principle, and this was another reason for the establishment of a separate Catholic Marriage Advisory Council. All the three organizations, the National Marriage Guidance Council, the Catholic Marriage Advisory Council and the Family Discussion Bureau, have remained in close touch with one another and their representatives continue to meet regularly.

In 1949, the Home Secretary set up a Marriage Guidance Training Board. The chairman and secretary of this board were appointed by the Home Office, and each of the three independent organizations nominated three members. The Ministry of Health and the Ministry of Education were also represented on the board. In the year before the board was set up, the Home Office made an emergency grant of £1,200 to the National Marriage Guidance Council. An annual grant of £5,000 was later made for the first period of three years, which enabled the Council to appoint a full-time officer to deal with the selection and training of marriage counsellors. This was Mr Alan Ingleby, and he was given the title of Education Secretary of the Council.

The government grant enabled the National Council to continue with the development of its own scheme of selection and training, and to produce counsellors, but it did not provide local Councils with the necessary finance for doing their work. However, local Marriage Guidance Councils had already raised substantial sums so that suitable premises could be rented and equipped, and the Home Secretary said that it was now their duty to approach local authorities for grants in aid.

The Council had begun, and was maintained, on a nonsectarian, non-political basis and, with the exception of Roman Catholics who joined their own organization, received support from members of the many other Churches in England and Wales. Leading members of the Jewish community in London approached the Council, with the result that several Jewish counsellors joined the London Marriage Guidance Council. The London Council also received the help of a Rabbi and a Jewish psychiatrist and lawyer. Council members also included people who professed no religious faith. The Council owes much of its subsequent success to the willingness of people of all and of no religious beliefs to help and support its work; this applies as much to the members of local committees as to the counsellors themselves. Many counsellors, of course, do their work because of their religious belief, but it is no part of their function to explain this belief to their clients, still less to attempt to make converts.

The Council's total income in 1950 was £9,000, and by 1955 this had risen to £16,500, although in 1952 the government grant had been cut for reasons of national economy from £5,000 to £2,500 for one year, resulting in members of staff having to accept temporary reductions in salaries. Nevertheless, the steady increase enabled more appointments to be made at the London Headquarters of the Council; Dr David Mace had left for the United States in 1949, to be replaced as general secretary by Mr Joseph Brayshaw, and in 1951 Mr Pestell, who had by then been secretary of the London Marriage Guidance Council for two years, was released by them and appointed field secretary of the National Council. As field secretary Mr Pestell (now Lord Wells-Pestell) became responsible for the founding of new Marriage Guidance Councils in many parts of the country, and also for the assessment of the work of all counsellors who had been operating for more than a year after finishing their basic training. This system of tutorial assessment has steadily developed since that time, and all newly trained marriage counsellors now have the regular support of paid tutors, who have themselves been selected and trained for this specialized work by the National Council. Tutorial support of counsellors in training is a very necessary safeguard for, in spite of the care taken at selection and during the basic training course, there are some people who are not able to benefit fully from the training and who have to be asked to withdraw from marriage counselling work.

By 1956 there were eighty recognized Marriage Guidance Councils in England, Wales and Northern Ireland, and it was the representatives of these Councils who made up the National Council and who elected a National Executive to run its affairs. Annual conferences were regularly being held, the first having taken place in Hertfordshire in 1947, and over 8,000 marriages a year were being helped by the counsellors. Almost 800 counsellors had attended the basic training course and the Council's work had become well known to the public.

The recommendations of the Denning Committee in 1947 had resulted in the Council's receiving its first grant, and in 1951 the new government appointed a Royal Commission on Marriage and Divorce. The Commission's report was published five years later, in 1956. The National Marriage Guidance Council had submitted evidence to the Royal Commission, which accepted the great majority of its recommendations. The Commission, dealing with the steadily rising tide of divorce, stated in its Report:

'We are convinced that the real remedy for the present situation lies in other directions: in fostering in the individual the will to do his duty by the community; in strengthening his resolution to make marriage a union for life; in inculcating a proper sense of his responsibility towards his children. These objectives can only be achieved by education in the widest sense, by specific instruction before marriage, and by providing facilities for guidance after marriage and for conciliation if breakdown threatens.'

The 'present situation' referred to by the Commission was a divorce rate of 26,265 a year, and in its Report it went on to make several specific comments on the need for support of the agencies providing marriage counselling, as follows:

'We strongly support the provision of greater facilities for marriage guidance and conciliation, and we make specific recommendations for the encouragement and development of work in this field.'

'We have already indicated the importance to society of bringing estranged spouses together. The State has thus an interest in furthering reconciliation wherever possible. We suggest that it would be unwise to attempt to define any formal pattern of conciliation agencies, or to set up an official conciliation system. The State's role should rather be to give every encouragement to the existing agencies, statutory and voluntary, engaged in marital conciliation . . . '

'It is our hope that a really marked extension in the work of education, pre-marital instruction, marriage guidance and reconciliation would check the tendency, to which we have referred, to resort too readily and lightly to divorce. Unless this tendency is checked, there is real danger that the conception of marriage as a lifelong union of one man with one woman may be abandoned. This would be an irreparable loss to the community.'

'We consider . . . that financial assistance to marriage guidance agencies is of such importance that local authorities should receive greater inducement to make contributions . . . '

'Facts learnt by a marriage guidance counsellor in the course of conciliation work should be inadmissible as evidence in subsequent matrimonial proceedings between the spouses.'

Apart from the very welcome recognition of the Council's work contained in the report of the Royal Commission, there was also a considerable increase in the government grant, which in the following year rose from £5,000 to £10,000. At the same time, the Home Office, acting on another recommendation of the Commission, sent a letter to all local authorities, calling their attention to the work of the marriage counselling agencies and encouraging them to make grants towards the expenses of these centres. Such grants could at that time only be given with the consent of the Minister of Housing and Local Government, under the terms of Section 136 of the Local Government Act, 1948. In 1959, the Ministry of Housing and Local Government wrote to the local authorities, informing them that the Minister had given general approval to grants to these agencies, of which the Marriage Guidance Councils were named as one, and in fact such grants have steadily increased from year to year. At the present time the total of these grants exceeds £50,000 a year. It was particularly significant that both the Denning Committee and the Royal Commission recommended that state support should be given to the existing agencies engaged in marriage counselling, and that it would be unwise to institute any system of state conciliation. These recommendations were of course made in the knowledge that there already existed a Probation Service, whose members undertake a nation-wide matrimonial conciliation service as a part of their duties as officers of the Courts.

Increased impetus was also given by the Royal Commission's report to the educational work of the Council, which had already begun to develop. As early as 1947 marriage counsellors had been invited to visit schools and youth clubs, and had begun to organize marriage preparation courses for engaged couples, usually in co-operation with the local churches. In 1955 Mr Ingleby began to devote all his time to the development of this education work and the Council appointed a training officer, Mr John Wallis, to continue and develop the selection and the basic training of marriage counsellors.

Another major activity of the Council, begun in 1945, was the production of publications intended for people who were married or who had marriage in mind. These covered many aspects of family life and were first produced at 6d per copy, attracting a good deal of attention in the national press. The first of these publications was entitled How to Treat a Young Wife, and it was given publicity by a national magazine; within a few weeks over 5,000 copies had been sold and this encouraged the Council to produce other booklets. The Council managed to find space for a book room at its already cramped headquarters in Duke Street, where at least one senior member of the staff was to be seen scrubbing the stairs at weekends, since there was not enough money to pay a regular cleaner. In 1953, the Council appointed a publications secretary, Mrs Angela Reed, who initiated the production of a popular series of booklets for young engaged and married couples and also made considerable improvements in the form and content of the Council's Annual Report.

Since 1947 the Council had been producing a monthly bulletin entitled Marriage Guidance, David Mace being the first editor. For many years this bulletin carried news from the various Marriage Guidance Councils and also articles of general interest. Notes on legal decisions occasionally appeared, as well as medical articles and a certain amount of correspondence. It also carried a small amount of advertising. In 1964, after a reorganization of the Council's administration, it was decided to produce two separate publications. The bulletin became a journal, published bi-monthly, and now contains a high proportion of articles of professional interest. A monthly newsletter is also produced and sent to all counsellors and other interested members of local Marriage Guidance Councils. Both are edited by Mrs Reed. The change was an immediate success and the journal received widespread publicity in press, radio and on television. It now carries substantially more advertising material and the monthly newsletter, also the responsibility of the publications department, has taken the place of a series of circular letters that used formerly to go out from the various administrative and technical departments at the London headquarters.

As a result of a special grant from the Carnegie United Kingdom trust, a book entitled *Marriage Counselling* was published in 1958.[1] The authors were John Wallis and H. S. Booker, the latter being Senior Lecturer in Statistics at London University. The book was divided into two parts, the first describing the development of the selection and training methods of the Council, and the second being an analysis of some of the cases seen by the marriage counsellors in the years 1952, 1953 and 1954. The first half of the book was later published separately under the title *Someone to Turn To*.

The lease of the National Council's premises at No. 78 Duke Street was due to expire in 1960, and by 1958 the offices had become extremely overcrowded. The national executive had given a lot of consideration to this problem and decided to search for new and much bigger premises. A building then occupied by the Royal College of Obstetricians and Gynaecologists, No. 58 Queen Anne Street, London, was found and it was decided to buy it. There was insufficient money available to enable the Council to do this, so it was decided to launch a national appeal for funds. The appeal committee was headed by Mr Paul

[1] London, Routledge and Kegan Paul.

Cadbury, chairman of Cadbury Brothers Limited, who was already treasurer of the Council and was later to become chairman of its National Executive. The appeal was organized by Sir Douglas Veale. It was a considerable success, attracting support from individuals, companies and trusts, and from individual Marriage Guidance Councils all over the country. A sum of £90,000 was raised, and the Council was able to move into its new headquarters, establish a book shop on the premises and set aside a fund which helped to support its work for the next six years. The headquarters were formally opened by Queen Elizabeth the Queen Mother in 1961.

The success of this appeal made possible the expansion of the Council's work in several directions. The staff at the national headquarters steadily increased, and it ultimately became necessary to appoint four regional officers who cover respectively the midland, northern, south-eastern and western regions of the country. This steady expansion was closely related also to the considerable increase in the educational work of the Council in schools and youth clubs, but as this important work is not the subject of this book it is not described here.

By 1967 there were just under 1,000 marriage counsellors working in different parts of the country. The annual government grant had risen first to £17,500, then to £21,000 and £30,000, and in 1966 had again been increased to £42,000. In spite of these welcome increases it became necessary to appeal again to the public for money to enable the Council to carry on its work, and in the autumn of 1966 a second national appeal was launched. Although the country was at that time in a period of severe financial restriction, the appeal produced a total of £50,000.

Between 1964 and 1967, the Council reorganized its structure and created new departments to deal with the ever-increasing flow of work. Not only was there the demand for the selection and training of more counsellors, but the Council was invited to send representatives to international conferences and to give evidence to committees and commissions set up by the government to enquire into different aspects of family life. Marriage Guidance Councils had been set up on a similar pattern at Sydney and Melbourne in Australia, at Christchurch in New Zealand and at Durban in South Africa. A Council was started in Israel, three out of its first four counsellors being British. The Council's work also had a considerable influence on similar organizations in Europe, mainly through the International Union of Family Organizations. The Union, created in 1948, had decided to set up a Commission on Marriage and Marriage Guidance, and David Mace, by this time living in the United States and working as executive director of the American Association of Marriage Counselors, became the first president of the Commission. The Marriage Guidance Commission has been addressed at different times by officers of the National Marriage Guidance Council, and many members attending its meetings have returned to their own countries to set up conciliation agencies designed to help marriages which have got into difficulties.

Another result of the reorganization that took place in 1964 was the creation of a field department, through which attention is now given to the administrative and practical needs of local Marriage Guidance Councils. A national secretary was appointed to have overall responsibility for both administrative and field work. Other departments were set up to provide tutorial assessments and other forms of in-service training for counsellors engaged in marriage counselling and in group discussions with young people. Training officers were appointed to supervise this work and to deal with the selection and basic training of all counsellors. The Council established a common form of selection for all its counsellors in 1965, and in 1967 altered the two forms of basic training that had previously been used to produce marriage counsellors and education counsellors. The basic training now equips all counsellors to work with individuals or with groups, according to their preference. Many prefer to do both types of work.

The majority of the Marriage Guidance Councils that have now become established in England, Wales, Northern Ireland, the Channel Islands and the Isle of Man are situated in the urban areas, but a few of them are serving large country districts. The National Council co-ordinates the work of all these local Councils and would have no existence without them. Each local Council aims to provide the three main services of marriage counselling, education counselling and the distribution of publications in their own community, and they depend on this community for their existence. In the early years, when the Council's work was first becoming established, some local Marriage Guidance Councils were not able to maintain an effective service and were forced to close down. This risk of closure was, and still is, accepted by the National Council as a necessary evil, for it has always been thought better that a local Council should stop work than that it should provide a poor or ineffective service. Such closures do, however, have an unfortunate effect on the Council's name in the locality, and it is often many years before an attempt can be made to establish a new Council.

In the great majority of areas, however, the tendency has been for Marriage Guidance Councils to expand steadily. Most of them now have adequate premises of their own where the marriage counselling work is carried on. In the large towns it has been found essential to have paid staff to run the service, the volume of work being too great for voluntary workers to handle. In addition to calls and enquiries, there is a large volume of correspondence to be handled. There are also records to be kept, and reception duties. In most towns the premises of the local Marriage Guidance Council are situated centrally, and clients can reach them fairly easily from the railway stations and bus routes. This is particularly important in country areas, where counsellors tend to be especially busy on market days.

Some of the larger Councils have set up outpost counselling centres, partly to help the clients who live in outlying areas, and also because it is more easy for the counsellors who live some way outside the main town to go to the outpost centre than to the main centre. Appointments are usually made by the appointments secretary at the main centre, as it is wasteful of time and money to have several people making appointments for the different centres. The same standards are set for the outpost centres as for the main centres, and clients can normally expect to be seen in comfortable surroundings in rooms which have an informal atmosphere rather than that of a clinic or an office.

It sometimes happens that members of a town council feel that their town should have a counselling centre, or even a separate Marriage Guidance Council, of its own. Whether this will be possible depends not only on the need that exists, but also on the recruitment of counsellors and on the support for the Council's work in the community. It is for these reasons that some fairly large towns in England and Wales still have no counselling centre. The National Council would like to see the work established wherever there is a need for it, but can only encourage the creation of new Councils where there is both the will and the means to do this. The support of existing Councils, and investigation into the ways and means of setting up new ones, is the responsibility of the field department of the National Council and it is mainly carried out by the regional officers.

It is difficult enough to recruit counsellors, especially in the large urban and industrial communities, but local Councils have also to find people willing to administer their work and to see that the three main services are maintained. No local Council can become a constituent member of the National Council until it has shown that it can offer an effective service. All Councils must also appoint at least one psychiatric and one legal adviser, and be able to operate on a sound financial basis. Community support for the work of the local Marriage Guidance Council is normally most clearly shown through grants from the local authorities. It is also most important for Councils to have the co-operation and support of the professions and of the other local social services.

Marriage Guidance Councils are usually started by a small group of people who have come into contact with the results of broken marriages through their own work. Councils have resulted from the initiative of the local branch of the British Medical Association, the probation service, the clergy and Rotary. Sometimes the proposal has come from the local authority itself and occasionally from one individual, the mayor or the town clerk. The first step towards the foundation of a new Council is to make contact with the National Marriage Guidance Council which then sends one of its regional officers to the area to discuss with the interested group the best way of setting about the work. Sometimes there is already an existing Marriage Guidance Council nearby, in which case that Council is encouraged to extend its services to the new area, relying on local support for the provision of premises, finance and particularly counsellors.

In some areas, however, it is established that there is a need but that there are no means of meeting it from one of the existing Councils. The local group are then encouraged to enlarge their numbers as necessary so as to be representative of the whole community, and to call a private meeting where the aims and methods of the Marriage Guidance Council can be explained and any questions answered. It is best to have this first meeting by private invitation rather than to hold it in public, for some matters under discussion are of a private nature and any objections to the establishment of the Council are best voiced in a setting where they will not be reported in a sensational manner. Normally the chairman of the first meeting will be a prominent local personality, and the meeting will be addressed by one of the officers of the National Council. His task will be to explain the policy of the Council, the methods of selection and training, the means of financial support and the normal links with the professions and the other social services. He will also answer any questions that arise.

If there are any misunderstandings about the nature and the aims of the counsellors' work, these can be cleared up. The national officer has not only to explain what a Marriage Guidance Council will do but also to assess the degree of support that the intended local Council will have. If he concludes that only a minority feels there is a need for a new Council, he will try to discourage the group from setting up a Council at this stage, but instead suggest to them that they should work on until they can convince others. On the other hand, if it seems to him that the invited meeting fully supports the proposal to set up a Council, he will encourage the chairman to obtain authority from the meeting for the establishment of an exploratory committee, the nucleus of which will usually be the group who has called the meeting.

The exploratory committee normally has to work steadily for a year or more before it becomes clear whether a Marriage Guidance Council can be formed. Financial support has to be assured, premises found and members and potential counsellors recruited. The professional advisers have to be approached, and arrangements made for the making of appointments and for the other social services to be aware of the existence of the new Council. There are inevitable delays between the first meeting at which it is decided to establish a Council and the day when the first counsellor is able to start work. In the first place, candidates sponsored by the new Council have to pass the national selection process and then commence training. Some new Councils have been so unfortunate as to have none of their sponsored candidates accepted in the first year. When this happens it is extremely discouraging; the members of the new exploratory committee may tend to feel that the National Council is setting unreasonably high selection standards, and a visit by one of the regional officers is usually necessary.

Assuming, however, that the first counsellors have been selected, have started training and that premises have been found where they can see clients, the exploratory committee will now make contact with as many organizations as possible, informing them of the progress made, and will approach the local authority, if it has not already done so, for a grant to assist its work. A public meeting will then be called to report progress and to hear a statement of plans for the future. Another speaker from the National Marriage Guidance Council is usually invited to address this meeting, which will be reported in the local press. It is usually possible at this stage to recruit a large number of members for the new Council, each of whom is asked to contribute a small annual subscription. In due course a meeting of these members is held to adopt a constitution and to elect an executive committee to carry on with the work started by the exploratory committee.

Another function of the first meeting of members is to appoint the chairman of the Marriage Guidance Council, also the secretary and treasurer. A president and vice-president may also be appointed. From the first moment that it becomes generally known that a Marriage Guidance Council exists, clients will begin to come for help. Even in areas where it has been doubted whether there is a need, it is always found that the counsellors are fully extended in meeting the demands upon them, so the committee must see that the first impetus is maintained and that the counsellor recruiting programme goes on. They must also consider the best means of selling and distributing publications to those who need them.

The local Council must also appoint a secretary. In the early stages he or she is usually a volunteer, dealing with correspondence and enquiries, and taking the minutes of meetings of the Council and of the Executive. The secretary has to know everyone connected with the Council and needs to understand something about the work and functions of the counsellors. The National Council publishes a handbook for secretaries entitled *Running a Marriage Guidance Council*, which contains information about all aspects of administration of a local Council. It is printed in loose-leaf form so that sections can be altered and replaced from time to time. There are sections on the functions of all the officers of the local Marriage Guidance Council and especially on the work of the secretary. Communications from the National Council are sent to the local secretary, who has to complete an annual return of the Council's work. The National Council bases its national statistics on these returns.

It has often been found that Councils need an honorary secretary as well as a paid secretary, the latter referring executive decisions to the former. One sign that a Marriage Guidance Council has begun to develop a satisfactory service is that it has become necessary to employ a paid secretary, at first usually on a part-time basis. It is often possible to persuade local authorities to give grants to enable a paid secretary to be appointed. Some authorities, though not all, find it easier to make this kind of grant than a payment to cover the expenses of the volunteer counsellors. No doubt the reason for this is the lingering suspicion that attaches in some places to voluntary work, a legacy from the days when some voluntary workers earned the title of 'do-gooders'. Normally, however, an explanation of the standards of selection and training of counsellors is enough to remove this prejudice.

All local Councils need to have a treasurer to deal with the finances of the Council. Frequently, a local bank manager or accountant can be prevailed upon to take on this task, which is not onerous but which does require specialized skill. It is not simply a matter of receiving money and making payments in connection with the Council's business; applications for financial grants have to be made and these sometimes involve a visit to the offices of the local authority. Furthermore, the treasurer is expected to prepare a budget each year so that the Council's work can be planned. He also draws up the accounts at the end of the year, and these are independently audited. The handbook, *Running a Marriage Guidance Council*, gives details of alternative methods of preparing accounts and makes suggestions for budgeting and ways of approaching local authorities for help. One argument frequently used to the authorities is that the saving of marriages can prevent considerable expense in taking children into care. It costs over £500 a year to look after a child in a local authority home.

It is not only to the local authorities that the Council looks for financial support. Most Councils stipulate that a minimum fee of ten shillings be paid by individual members and two guineas by corporate members. Some Councils receive grants from local charities and also from large firms and businesses. It is generally accepted that the employee who is happily married is likely to stay in his job and to work satisfactorily, but that the man with troubles at home tends to move from job to job. Personnel managers of large firms and businesses frequently send members of their staff to see a marriage counsellor.

Other sources of income for the local Council are the functions organized by committee members. These range from dances and concerts to fashion shows, coffee mornings and jumble sales. All this voluntary income is valuable, not only in financing the work done by local Councils, but in showing the local authorities that this work is supported by the community and that their members are able and willing to help themselves.

It has already been stated that the National Marriage Guidance Council consists mainly of the representatives of its constituent member Councils. These members normally meet twice a year, in the spring and autumn. In May the Council holds an annual conference which includes its annual general meeting, and this conference is attended by upwards of 300 people. The form of these conferences alters from year to year, but there are usually papers read by visiting experts on matters of general interest relating to marriage and family life. Private sessions of the conference also include discussions on topics of current interest in which members can join. As the Council has steadily grown larger and larger it has become more difficult to retain the atmosphere of the earlier days when almost all the delegates knew one another. On the other hand, the press and other mass media have given increasing attention to the Council's conferences. In 1967 the annual conference was addressed by the Lord Chancellor, Lord Gardiner, who was formerly a member of the Legal Advisory Board of the Council, and his speech on the need for divorce law reform attracted considerable national publicity.

Chapter 2

THE COUNSELLORS

Marriage counselling for a recognized Marriage Guidance Council is done only by counsellors who have been selected and trained by the National Marriage Guidance Council. At some Marriage Guidance Councils there are as few as two or three counsellors, and at a very few there are more than fifty. The great majority of counsellors are unpaid, and their clients are not charged any fee for the help they receive.

The Marriage Guidance Council has found over a period of more than twenty years that people under thirty are, with very rare exceptions, not mature enough for marriage counselling work. Even some of those between thirty and thirty-five have been found to be insufficiently developed. At the other end of the age-scale, people much over fifty who have not had any experience of counselling or of similar work are not likely to be able to make the necessary adjustments in training. For these reasons the Council encourages its constituent Councils to sponsor people, where possible, between the ages of thirty and fifty. This policy sometimes is misunderstood, particularly by those outside this age range; speakers are often asked why the Council has 'set a rigid age limit' for acceptance of candidates for the work. In fact, no arbitrary limit of any kind has been set, but experience has shown over a period of years that those people most likely to be selected are within the intermediate age range of thirty to fifty years.

There is no insistence on any particular academic or professional education, but candidates have to be of at least average intelligence and therefore able to benefit from the basic training course. Counsellors are naturally expected to be of good reputation and of high integrity; clearly these are vital elements in confidential work of this kind. At one time the Council did not accept divorced persons as marriage counsellors, but this policy was altered in 1965 and today any individual, married, single or divorced, can be sponsored by a Marriage Guidance Council, although Councils are under no obligation to sponsor a divorced person, or indeed any person, if they do not want to do so.

Counsellors work as part of a team, and are responsible in the first instance to their local Marriage Guidance Council. The National Marriage Guidance Council is responsible for selection and training, and for supervision of the standards of work both during and after the basic training. Counsellors have therefore to be acceptable both to the local and the national Council; this system operates very well, and results from the autonomous status of local Councils. The national executive can, however, decline to accept as a new constituent member of the National Council any Council that is not offering an effective service to the community. Local Councils appoint a representative to act as a member of the National Council, which elects the national executive through a system of regional representation.

Most counsellors are, or have been, happily married, and by far the largest proportion of them have children. Indeed, it seems that counsellors' families are rather larger than average. Certainly they are people who have had a good experience of relationships with others, and are free from undue prejudice. One quality that least fits a marriage counsellor is the conviction that he knows what is right for other people. Telling clients to 'pull themselves together' or to stop worrying is quite unhelpful, because their problem is often that this is just what they cannot do. Suggestions of taking action that is beyond the client's capacity only depresses him. On the other hand, the capacity to accept other people as they are, and to understand their problem as they feel it, is of fundamental importance in marriage counselling. It is this capacity, among others, for which the selectors look at the selection conferences run by the National Council.

The first and constantly recurring problem at almost every Marriage Guidance Council is finding enough counsellors to meet the constant requests for help. The net has to be cast wide in the community, and it is of little value to try to recruit counsellors from one social class, one political or religious group, or one sex alone. Counsellors both can and should be drawn from all sections of the community. Success in recruiting counsellors will naturally depend on the area in which the Council operates. It has been found, for instance, that it is particularly difficult to recruit counsellors in the new towns that have been built in

Britain in the last fifteen years. Marriage Guidance Councils in these areas usually have to go out to the surrounding towns and villages to find candidates for the work.

The problems of finding suitable counsellors are by no means confined to the new towns. Counselling involves giving up a lot of time, undergoing a fairly lengthy and demanding selection procedure, and then taking part in the basic training and in-service training programme. Counsellors are also required to keep regular case notes and to attend case discussions. This is done without financial reward, and it is by no means everyone who has both the time and the inclination to do it. It is perhaps surprising that over 700 people a year attend selection conferences, and that there are presently about 1,000 counsellors working in the 122 Marriage Guidance Councils in different parts of the country. On the other hand, one of the reasons why some counsellors were first attracted to the work was the high standards that the Council set. For them, the selection process represented something of a challenge. It has been stated that the great majority of counsellors are unpaid. In 1968 an experimental scheme was started by the London Marriage Guidance Council under which a small number of counsellors now receive payment for their counselling work on a sessional basis. This scheme is being operated in close association with the National Council.

It has been found that the most successful way of recruiting people to work as marriage counsellors is to make a personal contact with them. There are of course dangers in this; if a friend of someone connected with the Marriage Guidance Council has been persuaded to go forward for selection and has not been selected, this can cause embarrassment between them. Only if the nature of the selection process has been explained and accepted can this be avoided. Another effective method of recruitment is for the Marriage Guidance Council to send speakers to local groups to describe the aims and work of the Council. This often results in volunteers offering to help the Council in one way or another, some of whom become counsellors. The National Council also has a national recruitment programme through the press, radio and television, and directs enquirers to the Marriage Guidance Council nearest to their home.

As previously explained, members of the Roman Catholic faith who wish to undertake marriage counselling work, and are suitable for it, join the Catholic Marriage Advisory Council, and there is a Jewish Marriage Education Council that undertakes education and marriage preparation work, and some marriage counselling work, among orthodox Jews. Nevertheless, there are many Jews working as counsellors, and helping in other ways, at Marriage Guidance Councils. Counsellors come from most of the religious communities in this country, but of course many of them profess no religious faith. A counsellor's beliefs are very relevant to his motives for doing the work, but they are not discussed with the client.

One very effective way of appealing for counsellors is through the columns of the local press. To aid recruitment, all potential counsellors are sent leaflets describing the work and prepared by the National Council. Naturally, not everyone who replies will be suitable and on further enquiry some people decide not to go ahead, but there still exists the opportunity to enlist their help in some other capacity on behalf of the Council. One difficulty with letters written to the press is that they tend to bring in a flood of additional clients, thus making the need for counsellors even greater. At one local Council, a letter to the press produced over twenty replies. Following correspondence and discussions, four of these people were sent forward to selection conferences, and one was selected. This is not an exceptional situation, and illustrates the difficulty of finding the right type of candidate. Other ways of recruiting counsellors include the distribution of leaflets to local organizations, and encouraging existing members of the Council to search for suitable people. Several new counsellors have come from among the receptionists and other workers who help from time to time at the premises of the Marriage Guidance Council. Contact with the clients, and with the counsellors, often causes these people to apply to the Council to be sponsored for selection.

Recruitment is only the first step. All volunteers have next to be seen by a sponsoring committee at the local Council, and by one or more experienced counsellors. The object of this sponsoring procedure is not only to give the Council the opportunity of assessing whether the candidate would be acceptable at local level, but also to give him or her the chance of seeing how the

Council works and the kind of people who are associated with it. Sponsoring, then, is a two-way process of inspection, and a great many people naturally fall out at this stage, not only because the Council may decide not to sponsor them but often because they feel, having learnt about the counsellors' work, that it is not for them. Many volunteers are put off by the amount of time involved in training, the necessity of keeping case notes, and the regular counselling sessions and tutorials. There was a time when it was said that the high standards set by the Council, and the amount of time involved, would tend to discourage the great majority of suitable and potential volunteers. In fact, it has been found that every increase in the amount of time spent in training has been followed by an increase in the number of volunteers who want to take it.

It sometimes happens that, for local reasons, a Council feels that it must sponsor a particular person as a counsellor, even though they have severe doubts about his or her suitability. This is quite understandable, for the people associated with the local Council know the candidate personally and may wish to avoid giving personal offence. They therefore leave it to the National Marriage Guidance Council to make the assessment, in the knowledge that the candidate is not likely to be selected. The advantages this gives at a local level are balanced by the clogging of the national selection machinery that results, and in 1966 a new form of selection was devised which has helped to reduce the size of this problem. Originally, selection conferences lasted twenty-four hours and involved an overnight stay at a selection centre. Selection has now been divided into two parts, and is no longer residential. This reduced the cost of selecting counsellors without affecting the quality of those selected, and also led to a shortening of the time taken between the day a counsellor was sponsored and the day he went to the first selection conference. The new selection process was not designed specifically to meet the difficulty of the long waiting lists for selection, but it has in fact helped considerably to do this. It was devised as an alternative, but equally effective, method of selection, and it is considerably less expensive to operate.

It can readily be understood that a national system for the selection of counsellors is greatly preferable to a local system. In the first place, the existing system enables a uniform standard to be set and maintained by the Marriage Guidance Council. Secondly, it would be quite inappropriate for people in a local community to decide that they were suited for this difficult and demanding work, simply because they wanted to do it.

At the sponsoring stage it is clearly explained to the candidate how much time he will be expected to give to the basic training, the in-service training and to the work itself. At least one weekly session of three hours is required of all counsellors in return for the training they receive. The National Council's view is that continual experience of the work is necessary if counselling is to be effective. As an example of this, if a counsellor has to stop work for a period of six months or more, he is asked to return and take part of the basic training course again. Writing up case notes will normally take at least an hour of the counsellor's time each week, and more time is involved in attendance at case discussions. It is vital for all these obligations to be explained to candidates at an early stage, otherwise they may go to the selection conference on a wrong assumption. It is still occasionally found at the selection stage that a candidate has not really the time to give to the work. This is frustrating for him, and leads to unnecessary delay in selecting those candidates who can spare the time for marriage counselling.

It has already been explained that selection takes place on two separate days, and these are normally spaced a few weeks apart. In the first place, the local Marriage Guidance Council has to send a sponsoring form to the National Council. This confirms that the candidate is acceptable to the local Council, and has the time for the work. It gives a private and confidential report on the candidate, normally signed by the chairman of the Council, and also the names of two people to whom the National Council can write for a reference. These references are taken up before the selection conference is held; the Council asks for confidential information of a very personal nature, the object being to discover what kind of person the candidate is, rather than the number of qualifications he has obtained. Referees are not merely asked to say whether the candidate is a respectable individual; they are given a short account of the nature and responsibilities of marriage counselling, and asked to give a brief note of the candidate's disposition. They are asked whether the candidate has a genuine interest in other people's welfare, and whether he can take a detached and balanced view of their personal problems. Finally, the referee is asked whether he can recommend the candidate without reservations of any kind.

It is obvious that, because of the personal and confidential nature of the references and of the whole selection process, no reasons can ever be given after selection why a candidate was not accepted, if such is the case. All candidates are told that anything they say to the selectors will be treated confidentially and that nothing will be reported to a referee, or even to the sponsoring Council, except the simple statement that the candidate has, or has not, been selected for training. This causes difficulties from time to time, as some Marriage Guidance Councils seem to be more successful than others in putting forward suitable candidates. One local Council put up twelve candidates without any success, while in another area eleven candidates were accepted within a period of three years. In order to resolve these difficulties, a section has been added to the Council's handbook, *Running a Marriage Guidance Council*, giving guidance to local Councils on the subject of recruitment, sponsoring and selection.

The prospective counsellor attends Part I selection on a day of his or her own choosing. Slightly more than two-thirds of the candidates sponsored are women, and the Council has found in the past that a slightly higher proportion of men than women are in fact selected. As a result of this, there are about twice as many women working as marriage counsellors as men. Part I selection is normally held at the premises of one of the larger Marriage Guidance Councils or at the London headquarters of the National Council. Nine candidates attend and are first asked to take a series of written tests, including an intelligence test. This is a very necessary part of the process, and sounds rather more alarming than it is. Most candidates, having finished this written work, are able to relax and enjoy the rest of the conference. They then have interviews with two selectors, while the conference convener goes through and marks the written work. The conference starts at 10 a.m. and ends at 4 p.m., but no candidate has to attend for the whole of this time, as the programme is arranged so as to release candidates as soon as is conveniently possible. People coming at 10 a.m. are able to leave after lunch.

As soon as the conference is over, the selectors discuss the candidates for as long as is necessary to reach a decision about each one of them. This sometimes takes a long time, but it is never done in a hurry. The Council naturally likes to select as many people as it can, but in recent years it has only been found possible to accept a little more than half of all candidates sponsored by local Marriage Guidance Councils at this stage. Candidates normally hear the result of the conference within a few days and, if successful at Part I, they are invited to attend a Part II selection conference. The National Council bears all the expenses of running these selection conferences, including meals, but does not normally meet the travelling expenses of the candidates, which are usually paid by the local Council which has sponsored them. No candidate need be prevented from coming forward on financial grounds, and help with travelling expenses can be given if absolutely necessary. At the same time as the candidate is informed of the selectors' decision, a letter is also sent to the secretary of the sponsoring Marriage Guidance Council. The local secretary is asked not to make it generally known if the candidate has passed Part I selection, for to do so can cause disappointment and embarrassment if he is not successful at Part II.

Part II normally follows about six weeks after Part I, and is usually held at an existing Marriage Guidance centre in one of the larger cities in the country. Selection conferences are arranged to meet the demand in different parts of the country and are held in London, in the north, the east and west midlands, the west country and on the south coast. There are naturally fewer Part II than Part I conferences, the number of candidates having been somewhat reduced by the second stage. At Part II, candidates have an interview with a psychiatrist and discuss imaginary cases in groups, observed by two other selectors. As selection is now for both marriage counselling and education work with young people, the situations discussed by the candidates will include face-to-face situations as well as the kind of problems that a group discussion leader will be likely to meet. Although for reasons of confidence the cases have to be fictional they are quite typical of those handled in practice by counsellors, and the candidates' reactions to them are most helpful to the selectors. At the end of the Part II conference, which all candidates attend from 10 a.m. to 4 p.m., the selectors meet and again discuss all the candidates individually until they reach a unanimous decision about each of them.

The selectors can come to one of three decisions: they can accept a candidate for training; they can decide that he cannot be accepted; or they can 'defer' him. This last decision is a direct invitation to the candidate to return to another selection conference after a period of one, two or three years, and it usually implies that the selectors feel that he is not yet ready for this kind of work, although he may well be ready for it in a few years. Most candidates who are deferred are young, around the age of thirty years.

It will be noted that candidates are selected 'for training'. This proviso is essential, as it sometimes happens that a counsellor in training is not felt by the tutors to be making progress. In these circumstances he may be asked to withdraw, after the reasons have been explained to him. The National Council always uses the term 'selected' or 'not selected', and deliberately avoids the term 'rejected' because rejection of the individual is not implied. There are some people, highly suitable for other work, who will not make effective counsellors, just as there are some on whom marriage counselling will impose too great a strain. It would be quite wrong to say that such people had in any sense been 'rejected'. A candidate can appeal against the decision of the selectors, on the grounds that it was not made fairly, and this appeal is considered by the training panel of the National Council; if upheld, the candidate will normally be asked to attend another selection conference.

After selection, counsellors go on to the basic training course provided by the National Council. As with selection conferences, counsellors are sent a list of training courses that are being held in various parts of the country and are invited to say which of these they find it convenient to attend. There are six sections comprising the full basic training course, each lasting two full days, and each section involves the counsellor having to stay away from home for two nights. The training is fitted into three terms a year which correspond with the school terms. This seems to suit counsellors best, because many of them have children of school age. Counsellors manage somehow to persuade their husbands, wives and relations to look after the house and children while they are away from home, and training courses are held either mid-week or at weekends. Everyone is agreed on the need to avoid Mondays, so courses normally start on Tuesdays, Wednesdays or Fridays. They begin at 4 p.m. on the first day and continue until the same time two days later. The training at each section is very intensive and is designed to stretch counsellors to the limit of their capacity. There are few breaks, except for meals, and sessions go on until late in the evening. In spite of this high pressure of work, it is quite normal for the counsellors themselves to continue with independent discussions late into the night. The training sections are universally enjoyed, in spite of the hard work involved.

The first section introduces the counsellors to the ideas, practice and problems of marriage counselling. By the time they arrive at the training centre counsellors will have already received a series of training booklets which supplement the courses. They will also have received training notes which are used during the training sessions. Counsellors have been asked to read through the appropriate training booklets and notes before each section and are given a list of essential reading, recommended reading and further reading, through which they will work as the basic training course progresses. The centres used by the National Council are situated in many parts of the country, normally being run as residential training or conference centres by other bodies. These centres may be owned and run by a local authority, a religious foundation or a large commercial company. Some training courses are held in hotels that are suitably situated and reasonably priced. Centres used include Birmingham, Sheffield and Pulborough, and the National Council has to spend a good deal of time and energy searching for suitable places.

Part A of the basic training, which counsellors must take before they start any marriage counselling work, is easier to experience than to describe. Counselling is not a matter of assessing other people's problems and then advising them on a course of action, although many people think that it is. Counsellors are trained to listen to people, to accept them as they are without trying to change them, and to help them find a way through their difficulties. This is a much more effective way of helping than to give advice on how to 'solve' emotional problems. It follows that if the first part of the training course were to include instructions on how to be an effective counsellor, this would give the impression to the new counsellors that a similar sort of directive could be given to clients on the way to solve their marriage problems. And so, Section A asks questions of the counsellors instead of answering them, and is designed to enable them to develop the skills, latent or otherwise, for which they were selected. No attempt is made to turn out a uniform type of marriage counsellor, although it is made clear at this stage of the training, and in the training booklets, that counselling is done on non-directive lines. That is to say, counsellors do not suggest to their clients what action they should take, but try rather to help them to understand themselves and to take their own decisions.

For many counsellors, then, section A is challenging, and for some it is rather frustrating as well. Whether they can develop into effective counsellors will depend on the extent to which they can adjust themselves to this new approach to people. The tutors are constantly helping them to do this, and are also watching to see whether or not they are responding to the training. If a counsellor does not seem to be benefiting from the training, the tutors will always discuss this with him, in the hope of resolving the difficulty.

There are of course some rules which counsellors are expected to follow. The first is to respect the confidences of the client. Nothing a client says to a counsellor is mentioned to anyone else without his or her consent. The only exception to this is that counsellors can discuss their cases with tutors, psychiatric and legal advisers to the local Marriage Guidance Council, or with their colleagues at regular case discussions. Cases are therefore discussed only with other trained colleagues, and in these discussions names are not mentioned. In particular, a counsellor will always decline to discuss the details of a case with a lawyer, however well-disposed he may be towards the work of the Council. Counsellors are told many facts which have a legal significance and, if they were to disclose these to solicitors, this would provide evidence that could be used in court proceedings. Very few clients would be prepared to see a marriage counsellor and discuss matters frankly with him if they thought that their confidences might later be repeated in a divorce court.

In Australia, and in some other countries, an accredited counsellor who has been attempting to effect a reconciliation cannot be called to give evidence in a divorce case, but this is not the law in Great Britain. A person involved in matrimonial proceedings can claim privilege in respect of any statements made to a counsellor in an attempt at reconciliation but, if he waives this privilege, there is nothing to prevent the counsellor being called to give evidence. It might be thought that in such a case there is no objection to the counsellor giving evidence, because it is with the consent and at the request of the client. However, the difficulty here is that it might become known publicly that the counsellor had given evidence and this would tend to prevent other people in need of help from seeking it, for fear that their confidences would not be respected. Fortunately, on the only occasion on which a counsellor was subpoenaed to give evidence at a divorce court, the commissioner hearing the case told her to stand down, as it was not in the public interest that she should be required to reveal what had been said to her. The counsellor concerned had attended at the court with her bags packed, ready to go to prison rather than repeat what she had been told. For some years the National Marriage Guidance Council has been pressing for the law to be changed so that marriage counsellors should be privileged from giving evidence in matrimonial cases. The Royal Commission on Marriage and Divorce, in its report published in 1956, recommended that this change should be made.

The national secretary of the Council deals frequently with approaches made to counsellors by solicitors, and is usually able to persuade them that it is not in their clients' interest to pursue the matter. Nevertheless, there are times when the enquiries are pressed further and when solicitors threaten to force counsellors to attend court. It is very much in the interests of marriage reconciliation work in Britain that an early change should be made in the law in this respect.

Counsellors frequently have occasion to discuss details of a case with a client's doctor, but this only happens with the consent of the client. The client often asks the counsellor to speak to the doctor, and the counsellor will do this unless he feels that it would be better for the client to take action for herself. Some clients have become so used to having other people do things for them, possibly since childhood, that they are unable to act for themselves, and it can often be a help if the counsellor discusses this with them, in the hope that they can develop sufficient independence to enable them to help themselves rather than rely on others to act for them. This principle applies equally when the client asks the counsellor to approach social workers or other professional people. There are, of course, some occasions when the counsellor does decide to get in touch with a third party if he feels that it will help rather than hinder the client and if he has first obtained the client's permission to do so.

Counsellors always confine their letters to clients to matters relating to appointments, and do not mention the details of a marriage problem in correspondence. Letters containing such details could later be produced during the course of legal proceedings, again giving the impression that the Council's work was not confidential and thus deterring other clients from coming for help. In the counsellors' training notes there are specimen letters that counsellors are recommended to write to their clients concerning interviews, or to the other partner, inviting him or her to see the counsellor. The only exception to this rule of omitting all details of cases from correspondence arises when the client has been referred to a psychiatrist with the consent of the client and of his doctor. In these circumstances the counsellor will make a note of the salient features of the case for the psychiatrist, and will tell the client that he is doing this.

Although the counsellor and client often get to know one another quite well, the counsellor does not normally give the client details of his own home address or telephone number. If there is to be a second or subsequent interviews, these are arranged between counsellor and client at the end of the previous interview. If the client wants to cancel an interview she will be asked to tell the appointments secretary of the Marriage Guidance Council, and not the counsellor. This is not only to enable the interview to be given to another client but also because it is normally unwise for the client to know where the counsellor lives. Many counsellors who have told clients where they live have had visits from them, or have been telephoned at awkward times.

In marriage counselling it is generally unwise for the counsellor to talk about himself and his family, because it simply does not help the client to do so. It is through the relationship built up between the counsellor and client that help is given, but the main subject of the interviews should be the client and her feelings, not the counsellor. There is always the possibility that the client may become closely attached to the counsellor, and when this happens the counsellor needs the help of his colleagues during case discussion. He will try to help the client discuss and work through these feelings, and this will be the more difficult if the counsellor has previously talked to the client about himself and about his own family or his job. Emotional involvement of the client with the counsellor can arise in many ways. The counsellor may come to represent the 'ideal' person whom the client feels she has always needed; this can happen irrespective of whether the counsellor is a man or a women. Alternatively, the client may place the counsellor in the role of the disapproving parent and become extremely hostile towards him. In either circumstances the counsellor should be able to accept and to understand the client's feelings without becoming embarrassed or resentful. It is much easier for the counsellor to do this with the regular support of case discussions with his fellow counsellors, and with the help of a skilled tutor.

Most counsellors, after completing part A of the basic training course, can start counselling immediately, and indeed they are encouraged to do so. It may be thought that this is rather early to allow the new counsellors to start work, but counselling is a skill that can be learned effectively only by being practised. The safeguard for the clients is first, that the counsellor has been most carefully selected for the work, and second that all counsellors have the support of a tutor throughout their counselling life, and most especially during the first two years while they are in training. During the remainder of the basic training course, considerable time is taken up by case discussions, during which the counsellors can bring in their first experiences with clients, obtaining help from their colleagues and from the tutors on the training course.

It has already been mentioned that the counsellors have agreed before selection to give at least one session of three hours a week for their counselling work. Most counselling interviews last for one hour, although the first interview may take rather longer than this. After the first interview, counsellors in training are encouraged to conduct interviews so that they do not extend beyond an hour, not only because this can cause inconvenience to the next client waiting for an interview, but also because the counsellor will need to make a few case notes. Another reason for limiting the length of interviews is that there are many clients who, because of their anxiety, would like to extend the interview beyond an hour. It does not really help them to allow this to happen, and clients soon get used to the idea that the interview lasts only an hour, particularly if the counsellor makes it quite clear at an early stage that this time cannot be extended. Many counsellors see clients who will talk volubly for the first fifty-five minutes, but who will only mention their deepest anxieties just as they are getting up to leave, or even as they have their hand on the door-knob. It is very easy in such circumstances to allow the interview to continue, but it does not really help the client, who may be tempted to extend later interviews in the same way so as to postpone talking about the things that are most painful to him. He does need to discuss these problems, and he should not usually be helped to avoid them.

Counsellors, as well as keeping to a reasonable time limit for interviews, will explain to the client, at an appropriate moment, the method of counselling used by the Marriage Guidance Council. Counselling is not a quick short-cut to a solution of the client's problem. The counsellor is offering a series of regular interviews over a period of some weeks or months. It is left to the client to decline this offer if he wishes to do so. Another difficulty that often faces new counsellors arises when their clients ask them to take some action on their behalf. For instance, the client asks the counsellor to get in touch with the local housing authority or with the probation officer, or even with the police. Such is the client's urgency that the inexperienced counsellor is often very much tempted to do exactly this, but in the great majority of cases it will be much more effective if the client can be helped to take action for himself. Frequently, the very fact that the client has not been able to take the necessary action is the reason why he finds life so difficult. To take action on his behalf will be to leave him in this state; it will not encourage him to help himself.

All these difficulties, and many others, are discussed and

explained on part A of the basic training course. Following a short period during which the counsellors will normally have started counselling, they attend section B, which deals with the group work that is being done in discussion groups with young people in schools and clubs throughout the country. Over 65,000 young people are being helped in this way each year but, as this book is concerned with marriage counselling, the subject is not developed here. Nevertheless, all subsequent sections of the basic training course do include training in group work.

Sections C, D and E of the basic training deal with the development of the human personality from childhood and through adolescence to adulthood. Several of these training sessions are led by a psychiatrist. Others are led by a lawyer, who introduces counsellors to the legal aspects of marriage counselling. There is of course no attempt to turn the counsellors into psychiatrists or lawyers; the training for these professions normally takes five or six years. What the tutors are trying to do is to enable counsellors to know when people they are trying to help need expert advice from someone professionally trained and qualified to give it. For example, many clients have personal and emotional problems that also have legal implications; when this is so, they need the help of a lawyer, and the counsellor will normally suggest that they seek the advice of their solicitor, if they have one. If not, they may be referred to the local Citizens' Advice Bureau, or given a list of local solicitors who are prepared to give help in matrimonial cases. These solicitors will either see clients privately, charging a fee for their services, or under the Legal Aid and Advice Scheme, in which case the client may or may not have to make a contribution to the solicitor's fee. A client may talk of her problems in a way that leads the counsellor to feel that she may need psychiatric advice or treatment. If so, he will suggest to the client that she should see her doctor and, if the client consents, will get in touch with the doctor about the possibility of referral for psychiatric help.

The counsellor always makes any referral to, or through, the client's existing professional adviser, if she has one. The solicitors and psychiatrists who help local Marriage Guidance Councils do so as advisers to the counsellors. If a client is referred to the psychiatric adviser to the Marriage Guidance Council, it is always with the prior consent of the client's own doctor. In fact, counsellors normally find that this consent is gladly given and when it is withheld it is for the good reason that the client's doctor wants her to see a psychiatrist of his own choosing.

Sections C, D and E of the basic training, which are linked together over a period of a year and are attended by the same group of trainee counsellors, also include a study of the work of the other social services, both statutory and voluntary. It is vital that counsellors should know something of the work of other social agencies in the community, and they are encouraged to take this study further by making direct contact with other social workers in their own area. This aspect of the basic training course is dealt with by professional social workers.

Tutors on the basic training course also explain human physiology and deal with the sexual problems in marriage that counsellors will inevitably encounter in their work. It is not only the clients who need information about the ways in which their bodies function. Counsellors will normally know the basic facts of human reproduction, but almost all of them have gaps in their knowledge which need to be filled before they can help the people they are going to see. In this aspect of training in particular there is a considerable amount of supplementary reading to be done. Counsellors are given a list of required and recommended reading for the whole basic training course, and most local Marriage Guidance Councils maintain a technical library for use by their counsellors.

Section F brings the basic training course to an end. This section covers the work of the other sections in outline, and also includes case discussions. There is further study of the psychological aspects of the work, and Section F also includes discussion of the spiritual aspects of counselling. While the Council has no particular religious affiliation, many clients need help with ethical and spiritual problems. Members of churches will normally turn to their own clergy with such problems, but only a minority of the population attend church regularly, and marriage counsellors frequently have to help them in this area. In the event of difficulty, marriage counsellors can usually turn for help to the spiritual advisers attached to their local Marriage Guidance Council.

The training given to new counsellors at the residential

centres is deliberately termed basic training. It could not be, and is not intended to be, designed to produce counsellors fully competent and experienced in all aspects of the work. For this reason, all counsellors are expected to take in-service training in the form of weekly or fortnightly case discussions with other counsellors, and to have regular individual tutorial sessions. At case discussions, which are normally led by tutors appointed and paid by the National Marriage Guidance Council, actual cases being handled by the counsellors are considered. Any details that are discussed are regarded as completely confidential among the counsellors themselves, and these discussions are not open to committee members of the local Marriage Guidance Council. Without the client's consent, cases cannot be discussed with other social workers. This rule sometimes leads to misunderstandings, but the Council feels that any such discussions would be a breach of confidence.

All forms of basic and in-service training are the responsibility of the National Council, and a training panel plans and develops policy on behalf of the national executive. This panel is responsible for the selection and the further training of the tutors who work and are paid on a sessional basis on behalf of the Council. The greatest value of the tutorial session for the counsellors is the insight that it enables them to develop into their own feelings about people, and their reactions to them. The clients are of course not present at case discussions or tutorial sessions, so the other counsellors and tutors cannot see and listen to them. The counsellor, however, is there, and he has some reason for bringing the case to the group for discussion. This reason, and the counsellor's anxieties in relation to the case, will be closely examined. Quite often, the first reason the counsellor gives for mentioning the case is not his real one, and this he may discover, perhaps somewhat to his discomfort, as the discussion goes on. In the same way, clients will often bring some specific but minor problem to a counsellor for solution when their real anxieties lie deeper. The object of the case discussion is to help the counsellor to see more clearly how he is involved and by helping him to aid his client as well. Counselling is the use of a human relationship, and the counsellor is one half of that relationship. Looked at in this way, it can be seen how it is more helpful for the case discussion to concentrate on the counsellor's problem than on the client's. During case discussion, other counsellors also receive help as they bring out and examine their own feelings, comparing them with those of the counsellor whose own problems are being discussed.

When the case discussion is led by the psychiatric adviser to the Marriage Guidance Council, as it sometimes happens, it will frequently take a rather different form. The counsellors may need to ask the psychiatrist specific questions arising out of interviews with their clients, and he will indicate the extent to which professional help seems to be needed. For instance, if a client seems to be suffering from delusions of persecution, the psychiatrist will be able to advise the counsellor on the treatment that may be necessary, and will indicate the type of information that the counsellor should give to the client's doctor with this in mind. The psychiatrist may also indicate whether it will be helpful for the counsellor to continue to see the client. Similar considerations apply when a counsellor is seeing a client who appears to have a legal problem; the legal adviser will help the counsellor to decide whether the client needs legal advice. Special arrangements have been made by the National Marriage Guidance Council with the Law Society to cover such cases and, if the client has no solicitor already acting for him, the counsellor may refer him to the Council's legal adviser for help. Alternatively, he may be advised to seek legal advice through the local Citizens' Advice Bureau, or direct from a local firm of solicitors.

Counsellors make regular notes of all their cases. These are kept on sheets especially prepared and provided by the National Council. The front sheet gives full particulars of the client, with details of her family, their ages and occupations, the number of children and other important details. The following sheets, and there may be many of them if the case goes on for a long time, record the progress of the counselling interviews and the counsellor's own impressions and feelings about what is going on. The notes are not solely a chronicle of facts, but also represent an attempt by the counsellor to disentangle from a mass of material, frequently repetitive, the feelings of the client about his family, his work, and about the counsellor. The notes of the opening interview are necessarily more detailed than those of later interviews, but however long a case continues the counsellor keeps careful, though not lengthy, notes about each meeting with the client. These notes are kept under lock and key in steel filing cabinets at the premises of the local Marriage Guidance Council. Only the counsellors and the secretary of the Council have access to these files, and only counsellors and tutors are allowed to read case notes. These rules are strictly adhered to, as it would be quite wrong to allow any other people, including the other voluntary workers associated with the work of the Council, to have access to confidential records.

The counsellor will go through his case notes from time to time, for this helps him to discern developments in the case, if there have been any. If there does not seem to have been any progress at all, the counsellor needs to examine his own approach to see whether he is in fact helping the client. Some clients tend to go over the same ground again and again. If they are unable to break this pattern, they may still be supported to some extent, but for many clients this sort of constant repetition may mean that the counsellor has missed something important and is in fact preventing the client from making progress. Counsellors, like clients, can easily find themselves going round in circles. The case notes help the counsellors and their tutors to realize when this is happening.

It only became possible for the National Council to start appointing tutors for all areas of the country in 1965. A tutor-training scheme was organized, and all new counsellors are now given the name of their tutor as soon as they start training. Within a short time of seeing his first clients, the counsellor will be able to talk his difficulties over with the tutor, who will see the case notes and help him with the work. The benefits of this scheme have already become apparent, and tutors give continual support to those counsellors who need it in the early stages of their work. In time, the Council hopes to be able to afford to employ enough tutors to organize regular fortnightly case discussions for every Marriage Guidance Council in the country, together with regular tutorials for all working counsellors. Before 1965 is was not possible even to provide regional tutors, and the field secretary of the National Council had the responsibility of assessing the work of all counsellors. With the great increase in the number of Marriage Guidance Councils, and of counsellors, this became an impossible task for one man, and in

1964 responsibility for tutorials and assessments was transferred to one of the two training officers of the National Council.

It sometimes happens, during the basic training course or as a result of tutorials, that a tutor feels that a counsellor is not proving as effective in his work as had been hoped. Every effort is made to help him, and any shortcomings are fully discussed with him. If the tutors feel that, in spite of all possible help, the counsellor's work is not of a high enough standard, then he is asked to withdraw from counselling. Fortunately this happens but rarely, but it is a very necessary safeguard and maintains the standard of the counselling work. This is necessary not only for the protection of the clients, but for the counsellors themselves, who may be placed under an intolerable strain if they cannot meet the demands that counselling makes on them.

At the age of sixty-five all marriage counsellors retire, unless their Marriage Guidance Council asks the National Marriage Guidance Council to assess their work with a view to their continuing for another five years. At the age of seventy all counsellors must retire, but most counsellors in fact stop work at age sixty-five. The initiative regarding retirement is thus left with the local Marriage Guidance Council and not with the counsellor, who is not always the best person to judge whether the time has come for him to stop work.

Counsellors are not expected to pay for the cost of their selection and basic training, which has been estimated to cost the National Council about £200 per counsellor. They are not obliged to contribute towards the cost of accommodation or food at the training centres, but many of them do so. In their day-to-day work the counsellors incur a certain amount of expense in travelling, postages and telephone calls, and it is the firm policy of the Council that these expenses should be repaid by the local Marriage Guidance Council. If it were not so, there would be some people who would not undertake marriage counselling work because they could not afford it. This risk must be prevented, and it is one of the strongest arguments in favour of grants from local authorities to Marriage Guidance Councils. For those few counsellors who both can and wish to make additional contributions to the Council over and above the time they are already giving voluntarily, it is always suggested that they should claim and be paid their proper expenses, and then at a later stage make a donation to the Council. Made in this way, the donation properly appears as part of the Council's income from voluntary sources.

For many counsellors, the experience of the training and of their counselling work brings about profound changes in their attitudes, in their careers and even in their own marriages. Counselling training is designed to make the counsellor look at himself, consider his own motives and his reactions to other people, and to come to terms with his reasons for wanting to become a counsellor. He learns that there are situations and emotions that bring great stress to bear on him, usually because they expose long-forgotten feelings of his own. Through the training he comes to understand himself better, and by this means is able to help the clients he sees.

Chapter 3

THE CLIENTS

The client arriving for her first appointment at the Marriage Guidance Council is tense, anxious and uncertain what to expect. Some clients think they are going to be asked to pay a fee; others expect to see several members of the Council, ranged round a table. In fact, the client will normally be welcomed by a receptionist at the premises of the Council, or possibly by the counsellor whom she has arranged to see. There will be no fee to pay. The first object of the counsellor will be to put the client at her ease. She must be able to sit down in a comfortable chair, given time to take in her surroundings and to assess the counsellor as a person. She needs to feel that here is someone who is interested in her as a person, who is willing to listen and who is in no hurry. The counsellor will usually ask her to start by explaining her story in her own words. It is not wise for the counsellor to start by filling in forms for, although records have to be kept, it is quite possible to obtain all necessary information during or at the end of the interview. If she is allowed to tell her own story in her own way, from the beginning and without interruption, the client will feel that she is thought of as a person and not as a case.

Most clients expect to be given some kind of answer to their problem. They imagine that the counsellor will listen to them, then sum up the problem, give appropriate advice or instruction and send them away to try it out. It is not uncommon for a client to tell the story and then sit back, folding her arms, saying 'Well, you're the expert. What ought I to do?' The counsellor feels rather taken aback by this, even though he expects it. His problem is that he knows it does not usually help people to provide this kind of solution to their problems. Practical problems are capable of being remedied by a practical solution, but emotional problems need a different approach. So the counsellor has to help the client to explore her problem, the reasons why it has arisen and how she feels about it. It may be necessary for counsellor and client to meet many times while this process of discovery continues. In the year 1967, the average number of interviews given in each case seen by counsellors was between three and four; this figure represents a fairly large number of single-interview cases, and an equally large number of cases in which the client is seen over a period of several weeks or months. It is quite normal for the counsellor to continue the interviews over a period of a year or more. Frequently clients will come once a week for many weeks, but the normal tendency is for the interval between interviews to lengthen as time goes on.

Some clients make only one visit to the Marriage Guidance Council. This may be because they have not received the kind of help they expected. They may have come in the hope of finding, or being given, a solution to all their problems in a single interview, and if this is so they are almost certain to be disappointed. It is for the counsellor to explain to his client that marriage counselling takes time, but some clients are at such a critical stage in their marriage that they do not feel able to wait for the kind of help that the counsellor can give. They feel, understandably, that something must be done or decided straightaway or not at all. Other clients come to the Marriage Guidance Council expecting to be given money, or under the mistaken impression that the Council operates in the same way as the Family Planning Association and will supply contraceptives. It is possible to give these people considerable help by referring them to the Family Planning Association, the Ministry of Social Security or the Citizens' Advice Bureau, according to need, and this is frequently done.

The client may well have come to see the counsellor because she has a problem that she is reluctant to discuss with her own professional adviser, her doctor or solicitor. When this happens the counsellor will nevertheless encourage her to see her own adviser, often giving her the reassurance that will enable her to do this. As already explained, the counsellor may also make direct contact with the client's doctor or solicitor. Contacts of this kind are the most frequent with the medical profession, for almost everyone in the country has a doctor, but by no means everyone has had occasion to consult a solicitor. Moreover, if the counselling is helpful it may well be that the client sees no necessity for legal action, and will have no reason to seek advice from a solicitor.

A counsellor will normally encourage the client to take action for herself rather than to do this for her. To give an example, a counsellor will not normally approach the local housing authority, the police or the Ministry of Social Security, even if the client has asked him to do this. Instead, he will help the client to see why it will probably be more helpful for her to take action for herself.

At some stage in counselling the client will decide not to return for another interview. She may feel she is receiving no help, or have decided to bring her marriage to an end. On the other hand, it will sometimes be because she has partially or fully overcome her difficulties. When this happens it is quite normal for the client to feel that she does not wish to see the counsellor again, for he represents a link with a period of her life that the client wants to forget. New counsellors have sometimes to be helped to see that this feeling is often a symptom of recovery, and not of ingratitude. Some clients find it very difficult to tell the counsellor that they will not be returning, for fear that this will annoy him or make him feel that he has not helped. It is for this reason that clients are always told, although they sometimes forget, that they are perfectly free to stop the counselling interviews whenever it suits them. For other clients there may come a point in counselling when they have been brought face-to-face with their real problems, and this may involve their having to think about themselves in a new way. This can be painful, and not all clients can cope with this stage in counselling. If this happens they may decide not to go on. This feeling is accepted quite naturally by the counsellor, and no pressure is brought on the clients to continue with interviews against their will.

Clients come from all social categories in society, and have very varying grades of income. The Marriage Guidance Council is therefore helping all sections of the community, although the clients coming to any particular Council tend to differ according to the part of the country in which they live. The clients who live in the suburban areas of London are as different from people in the industrial towns of the Midlands and the North as they are from those who live in agricultural communities. Nevertheless, the type of problems they bring tend to be fundamentally the same, involving a breakdown in the relationship between husband and wife. The symptoms of marriage breakdown tend to differ from place to place. In one area it is quite normal for an argument to end with a man beating his wife. In another, this sort of action would be far less likely and might well result in the wife going immediately to see a counsellor. Counsellors need to be aware of the attitudes and customs of their own area, and if they have lived there for some time this awareness will come naturally to them. If they move from one area to another they will acquire this information during case discussions with the other counsellors, and through practical experience.

There has been no recent survey in detail of the type of people who come for help to the Marriage Guidance Council but the late H. S. Booker, co-author with John Wallis of *Marriage Counselling*, undertook a study of this subject covering the years 1952 and 1953. He found that less than one quarter of the husbands in the cases seen were unskilled labourers, or unemployed. About one third of the husbands were classed as skilled workers or transport workers, and a little under 30 per cent were clerical workers, travellers, civil servants, professional workers and teachers. Of the wives involved in these same cases, only about one third were doing paid work, and most of this work was described as clerical or unskilled. Booker also reviewed the educational background of the clients; he found that almost one quarter had received the equivalent of a grammar school education, and that 5 per cent had received higher education. In the years 1952 and 1953 it was the wife who came first for the help of the Council in 58 per cent of the cases seen, and the husband in 37 per cent. In the remaining 5 per cent of cases, husband and wife came together. No similar research in such detail has been undertaken since 1953, but the impression of the Council is that the proportions are much the same at the present time, and this would be in line with similar experience in the marriage conciliation agencies operating in Scandinavia. In 1966, 38,901 interviews were given to wives, 23,223 to husbands, and there were 3,383 joint interviews, in all cases coming to Marriage Guidance Councils in that year. It is interesting that in Australia (see Chapter 5) the proportion of joint interviews is twice that in Britain.

Those who work for the Marriage Guidance Council are very often asked how successful their work is. If there were some means of measuring success it might be comparatively easy to answer this question, but it would first involve the invention of a means of measuring human happiness. The only satisfactory answer the Council can produce to this question is the steady growth in its marital conciliation work: in 1952, 6,666 marriages were helped, and by 1966 this number had risen to 18,267. The Council considers that this is the best evidence available that the work of its counsellors is effective.

There is also great public interest, not only in the relative success of the work of the Council, but also in the nature of the problems that are brought to the counsellors. Any counsellor will say that these seem to be infinitely varied. The symptoms of marriage breakdown do not, perhaps, vary a great deal. It is quite common for counsellors to hear of situations involving infidelity, cruelty and desertion. It is not unusual for them to meet clients who are mentally disturbed and who need medical treatment. Others come with complaints about the way that their relatives interfere wth the marriage, about the problems of bringing up children or about financial difficulties. There are, naturally, some clients whose problems are purely practical, and for them it is often possible to provide practical help. This is particularly true for young married couples who are having sexual difficulties in early marriage, and who are too embarrassed to go to see their doctor. The great majority of marriage problems, however, lie beneath the symptoms that the clients first mention to the counsellor. For this reason it is misleading, let alone difficult, to describe these symptoms in any detail. If counsellors are unable to see, and encourage their clients to see, that their marriage problems lie deep beneath their immediate difficulties, they will render very little help.

Clients vary greatly in the way they behave when they first come to see a counsellor. Some feel guilty at having come at all, and most feel embarrassed. Often this guilt or embarrassment will appear as diffidence, truculence, or as aggression. Very few people like to visit a counsellor and admit simply that they are desperately worried and that they do not understand what is happening to them. Instead, they almost always have a complaint to make about the way their partner is behaving. At first they usually blame their partner; in fact, when clients first start the interview by blaming themselves it is often because they are cloaking their own resentment against their partner, or because they want to enlist the sympathy of the counsellor. During counselling, clients very frequently try to manipulate the counsellor into taking action for them. Others expect the counsellor to persuade their partner to change his behaviour. Counsellors are trained to be most careful not to be drawn into a situation where they pass messages from one spouse to the other, or take sides in the argument. In spite of this, it is very difficult not to see the marriage through the eyes of the client, particularly if one is only interviewing one partner of the marriage. It is here that the tutorial sessions and case discussions are of help to the counsellors, for they are enabled to look at their own involvement with the people they are helping, and to correct the errors in their own work.

The Marriage Guidance Council has always used the word clients to describe the men and women who come to see the counsellors. It is not the ideal description, as clients are asked for no fee, but it is more appropriate than the term patients, which would imply that the Marriage Guidance Council provides some form of treatment. Most clients make their first contact with the Marriage Guidance Council by telephone, and all local Councils have their number in the local telephone directory under 'Marriage Guidance Council'. At the larger Councils the telephone is at the premises used by the Council, where there will be a receptionist or appointments secretary to deal with calls during normal business hours. In the smaller Councils the telephone number will be that of the appointments secretary of the Council, who takes all calls at her home and who keeps the appointments book there.

When a client seeks the help of the Council she does not know what to expect. She has probably had to screw up her courage to make the approach at all, and it is very important indeed that she should immediately feel accepted and understood. Often enough the client comes at the very last moment, when the marriage is breaking down or when the couple have already parted. Some clients feel that it is disgraceful to have to admit that this has happened, and this is one reason why so many people come so late. In fact, if more clients were able to come to see a counsellor when the difficulty began to be serious, there would be a greater chance of helping them to find a satisfactory solution. Fortunately, an increasing number of young couples are now approaching Marriage Guidance Councils for help within the first years of their marriage.

The personality of the appointments secretary is as important as that of the counsellors themselves, for there is nothing worse for a client than to be treated in an abrupt manner, or made to feel a nuisance. The appointments secretary of the Council gives the first impression to the client of what the Council is like, and is responsible for the atmosphere in which the counselling begins. She has not only to be tactful and understanding in handling the clients, but has to be able to cope with pressure from the counsellors as well. Almost all clients feel that they need help desperately and immediately. If possible, they want to see a counsellor the same day that they call, and some say that they cannot wait. At most Marriage Guidance Councils it is impossible to arrange an immediate appointment because there are waiting lists in nearly all areas. Counsellors are available on only one or two days a week, and there is such a shortage of counsellors in some areas that many people cannot be given an interview at all. It is of little help to put their names at the end of a long waiting list which may involve their having to wait for several months, and the appointments secretary will sometimes have to tell enquirers that they cannot be seen. At some Councils it is the practice to wait until a counsellor can take on another case, and allot the next client that calls to that counsellor. This is scarcely satisfactory, but it avoids the frustration and disappointment of the long waiting list. At Marriage Guidance Councils having these difficulties, frequent referrals are made to the probation service, who are themselves very busy but who handle a considerable amount of marriage conciliation work.

It sometimes happens that a client asks for an interview and that, before she can be offered one, she and her husband have already separated. This danger, which is often mentioned by clients coming to the Council for help, puts considerable pressure on the counsellors, and particularly on the appointments secretary. On the one hand are the clients, pressing to be seen; on the other are the counsellors, unable to take on more work.

Appointments secretaries, who are normally volunteers, have to be introduced gradually to this very difficult aspect of their work, and more than one has resigned in the past as a result of this kind of pressure.

Fortunately, not all Marriage Guidance Councils are as hard pressed as this, but it would nevertheless be possible for the National Council to use at least twice the number of counsellors now selected and trained. Counselling normally involves seeing the client once a week, and each case can represent more than one interview a week, if both husband and wife are being seen. It is not practicable for even the most experienced counsellors to take on a caseload of more than six or seven clients. If they try to do so the standard of their work tends to suffer, they become irritated and tired and, if they cannot then reduce their case-load, they will be likely to stop work altogether.

It is not only the difficulty of arranging appointments that faces the appointments secretary. Clients, once they have made a contact with the Marriage Guidance Council, often want to talk about their problem to the first voice they hear. Very few appointments secretaries are also trained as counsellors, but it is very hard for them to refuse to listen to what the client wants to tell them. Unfortunately, this will not help the client who often assumes that having told one member of the Marriage Guidance Council about her difficulties, others will also know about them. In particular, she will expect the counsellor she later sees to know about the problem. This will not be so, because counsellors are trained to obtain the story direct from the client and not from any third person. Therefore, although it is not always easy, appointments secretaries have to explain to clients that they are not themselves counsellors, but that they will make an appointment for the client to see a counsellor.

It is difficult enough to cope with the making of appointments and to avoid being treated as a counsellor, but the appointments secretary also has to deal with other problems. Some clients, already upset, become irritated when they find that they cannot be offered an immediate interview. It is not unusual for clients to become angry, demanding to see a counsellor and adding that they know the marriage counselling service is provided under the National Health Service. This is of course a mistake, the Marriage Guidance Council being a voluntary organization, but it does not help the client to receive a curt denial. Appointments secretaries need to understand that the aggressive behaviour of the clients is a symptom of their anxieties, and that they are just as much in need of understanding and sympathetic treatment as those who arrive in tears. Here again the Council faces the problem that it first met when considering the selection and training of counsellors. Like them, the appointments secretary and most workers for the Marriage Guidance Council are volunteers, and it is not always easy to find suitable people for the work. Just as some candidates for marriage counselling work mistakenly feel that the clients' problems can usually be solved by good advice, so there are would-be appointments secretaries who feel impelled to give advice to clients on the telephone. It is a part of the work of the field department of the National Marriage Guidance Council to help train appointments secretaries. This is done through the handbook *Running a Marriage Guidance Council*, through local training courses and conferences, and through the regional officers employed by the National Council. It is unfortunate that shortage of funds prevents a comprehensive training programme for these workers, but the four regional officers make a point of visiting each Council in their region as often as possible, and can usually discern when special help is needed by the appointments secretaries, the other administrative staff, or by the counsellors themselves.

Clients are referred to the Marriage Guidance Council by the other social services, both voluntary and statutory, and by the professions, but most of them come to the Council on their own initiative, having heard of its work through friends, or read about it in the advice columns of the women's magazines. A recent national survey showed that 94 per cent of those questioned had heard of the existence of the Marriage Guidance Council. The same survey also indicated general approval of its work, but considerable uncertainty about the identity of the people who organized it. About one quarter of the sample thought that the Council was an official organization, run either by the state or by local government, and only 13 per cent thought (as is the case) that it was voluntarily organized. A majority of the sample gave a wholly favourable verdict on the work the Council is doing, and knew that the counsellors received training for their work.

Referrals are also received from the Citizens' Advice Bureau, the Probation Service, the Family Planning Association, the hospitals, and from doctors, lawyers and clergy. The proportion of referrals made by different professions and services tends to vary from area to area: in one county the Probation Service attributed a drop of 50 per cent in its matrimonial caseload to the operations of the newly-formed Marriage Guidance Council, and was making many referrals. In another area there were signs of resentment by professional workers of the fact that marriage counselling was being undertaken by volunteer workers, and no referrals were made. A similar variety of attitudes is found with the professions: some doctors suggest to their patients that they should visit the Marriage Guidance Council, glad to be able to make use of the counselling service, and having too little time for long-term counselling work with their patients. Other doctors do not care to make referrals to people who have not had a full medical training.

Some referrals are now being made by the divorce courts. In 1967, a scheme was inaugurated under which counsellors selected and trained by the National Marriage Guidance Council would take part in an experimental pilot project at the divorce courts in London. The scheme had been developed following an approach to the National Council by the President of the divorce court, and had also been discussed with representatives of the Home Office, the Lord Chancellor's Department, the Law Commission, the court welfare officers and other agencies involved in marital conciliation work. The scheme operates only in respect of those divorce cases that have come to the court within the first three years of marriage. Under Section 2 of the Matrimonial Causes Act, 1965 it is laid down that a divorce petition can only be presented within the first three years of marriage if there are exceptional circumstances. The same Section of the Act requires the judge to consider whether in such cases there is any prospect of reconciliation, and it is under this provision that the scheme has been developed. In the initial stages, the scheme is to operate only in the London area.

If a judge considers that there is some prospect of reconciliation he will direct the senior court welfare officer to interview both husband and wife. This officer is normally in attendance at court, and has already had training and experience as a probation officer. Experience has indicated that it is only where people are willing to co-operate that there is likely to be any real hope of reconciliation, and the interview with the officer will give some indication of this. If he sees no chance of a reconciliation he will report accordingly to the judge, who may then decide to grant the divorce. If, however, the officer does see some hope of reconciliation he will either deal with the case himself, refer the parties to another welfare officer attached to the court, or call on the help of a trained counsellor especially chosen for the purpose by the National Marriage Guidance Council. If there are special circumstances, e.g. denominational, the husband and wife may be referred to some other appropriate person or body. For instance, if they are Roman Catholics they are likely to be referred to the Catholic Marriage Advisory Council.

If the parties have been referred to the National Marriage Guidance Council for help they will be seen at suitable counselling premises, and not at the divorce courts. Everything they say will be regarded as confidential, and will not be mentioned in court. Counsellors operating the scheme have the same facilities for case discussion with tutors of the National Council as they have in their other counselling work, and regular meetings are held with the senior court welfare officer to review progress of the pilot scheme. When counselling is completed, the result is reported by the counsellor to the welfare officer, and not direct to the court. The welfare officer reports to the judge on whether a reconciliation has proved possible or not, without going into any details, and so far as the Marriage Guidance Council is concerned this is an end of the matter.

It is too early to assess the results of this new scheme, but it is hoped that, even if many reconciliations are not effected, it will still be possible to help some couples to face the inevitable feelings of frustration and disappointment that follow the early breakdown of their marriage. The scheme in no way represents an introduction of compulsory reconciliation; clients will be seen only on a voluntary basis and will be completely free to return to see the counsellor or not, just as they please, and for as long a period as they wish.

There is now a much greater degree of acceptance of the value of the work of the marriage counsellor than was the case in the early days of the development of the Council. As the number of clients has grown steadily over a period of twenty years, and as more experience has been gained in dealing with their marriage problems, so has the public image of the Council improved. When first formed the Council set up several advisory boards, including a medical board, a legal board and a clerical board, and many people of national standing were persuaded to join these boards. The Council made a point of publishing details of the membership of these boards, and in particular made considerable use of the members of the medical board, obtaining their advice on matters relating to the training of counsellors and on the material included in its publications. The existence of these advisory boards and the willingness of the government to support the work of the Council through an exchequer grant have led to a steady improvement in relations between the Marriage Guidance Council, the professions and the other social services. Another factor in this gradual improvement may well have been the increasing number of wives of professional people who have been selected and trained to work as marriage counsellors.

The client, having made contact with the Council by telephone, by letter or by calling at the Council's offices, is given an appointment to see a counsellor. The appointments system is necessary to avoid the waste of time that would be involved in counsellors having to attend at the premises and wait for clients to call. In fact, there are so many people wanting to be seen in most areas that an appointments system is absolutely necessary. Nevertheless, there are some difficulties with the system: if a client does not turn up for an appointment the time given by the counsellor is wasted. Of all first appointments made it has been found that about 15 per cent are not kept. This figure does not include those clients who telephone to say that they will not be keeping their appointments. In spite of considerable efforts over the years it seems to be impossible to reduce this proportion of missed first appointments. There are some people who, having made an appointment, cannot face the interview. For others the marriage difficulty may have been eased by the very fact of an interview having been made, an acceptance that the problem is being faced. It is perhaps surprising how many people do not let the Council know that they will not be attending, but no doubt many of them feel guilty about their change of mind and would rather not face the embarrassment of having to explain it. Marriage Guidance Councils have devised various means of dealing with this problem of missed appointments. Some send out a note giving the time and date of the appointment, and a few also enclose a reply-paid card asking for confirmation of the booking. One Council is charging a nominal booking fee for the first interview, usually five shillings, but other Councils have not been prepared to ask clients to make any kind of payment for what they feel should be an absolutely free service. Counsellors find that it interferes with their relationship with the clients to have to collect money from them, and the task is therefore left to the office staff. All these methods have been known to reduce the number of missed appointments, but not to eliminate them altogether.

As soon as the appointments secretary has made the appointment with the client, she makes contact with the counsellor and confirms it with him or her. Most counsellors work at a regular day and time each week, so it is fairly easy to arrange appointments. Some counsellors do this regular weekly work, and also take on additional sessions when the waiting list begins to lengthen. The appointments secretary makes a note of all appointments in a diary, and when counsellors want to arrange to see their clients again they fix a suitable time and keep the appointments secretary informed. When one series of interviews has ended, the counsellor then lets the appointments secretary know that he can take on another client. The making of appointments can sometimes be complicated by the type of premises used by the Council. Some Councils have reasonably large premises, where several clients can be seen privately and in separate rooms at the same time, but there are other Councils which have the use of only one or two rooms. At these Councils the appointments secretary has to exercise considerable ingenuity to prevent appointments from clashing with one another.

The premises used by the Council will normally be near the middle of the town, and clients will be asked to come there to meet the counsellor at an arranged time. In the early 1950s only a few Marriage Guidance Councils had satisfactory premises, but within fifteen years the situation has changed very considerably, and there are now very few Councils without a place of which they have exclusive use. Clients are only visited in their homes in the most exceptional circumstances, when one partner is ill and when both husband and life have consented to the visit. The homes of the counsellor and of the client are basically unsuitable for counselling work, because it is extremely difficult to create there the right atmosphere for counselling. In the home of either counsellor or client there are liable to be interruptions, and this knowledge can unsettle both of them. If interviews took place in the counsellor's home there would also be distractions for the client, who might compare it—favourably or unfavourably— with her own home. Clients would not be able to relax and to talk freely in their homes, and the Marriage Guidance Council therefore uses its own premises, where there is no fear of interruption.

The atmosphere created in the premises used by the Council is most important, although of course the work done depends basically on the skill of the counsellor. The room in which the client will meet the counsellor need not be at all large, but it should be well decorated and comfortable, with a carpet, easy chairs, and pictures on the walls. It will not have the appearance of a waiting room, or of an office or clinic. Great emphasis is placed on this by the National Council, counsellors having found that a clinical atmosphere is unhelpful to their clients, who need to be put at their ease as much as possible. This is why it is important that a Council should have exclusive use of the premises in which the work is done. If the premises of some other social service or organisation are used, excellent though these may be for the purposes of that service, they do not seem also to be suitable for marriage counselling work. Another reason for the need for exclusive use of premises is that clients do not like to have to pass through another office in order to be seen by a marriage counsellor. There are other advantages: case records can be kept securely, a library maintained, a separate waiting room provided, and the office can be independently staffed. In one area a local Family Planning Association and the Marriage Guidance Council arranged to share a waiting room, but it was found that several clients were not willing to make a second visit to see the counsellors. This Council was eventually able to find better premises, which made a noticeable difference to the **average** number of interviews given to each case.

Councils try to avoid placing large notices outside their premises drawing attention to their work, because this can embarrass the clients. Some sort of notice is of course necessary, but it should be small and on a plate similar to those used by professional firms. Inside the premises there is usually a notice stating that the Marriage Guidance Council is a voluntary organization, not part of the National Health Service, and that any contributions towards its expenses will be most welcome. Only a very small proportion of the expense of running Marriage Guidance Councils is in fact met out of the contributions made by the clients, although some counsellors do receive substantial donations from them towards the cost of providing the service. There is no doubt that some clients like to be able to make a payment in return for the help they have received, particularly when the counselling is coming to an end. A payment can represent to the client a means of bringing the contact to a conclusion in a way that expresses gratitude, but is final.

In many places, local authorities have placed premises at the disposal of the local Marriage Guidance Council. In the new towns particularly these tend to be well situated and suitable for counselling work, although sometimes the rooms are not entirely sound-proof, which can cause embarrassment and difficulty. As has been explained, all marriage counselling work is strictly confidential, but it sometimes happens that husband and wife come to the premises for consecutive interviews with the counsellor and, unless the rooms are completely sound-proof, this has obvious disadvantages. The difficulty can often be solved by fitting an extra door to the counselling rooms, and by making sure that the carpets and curtains are thick enough to absorb the sound of voices. Ideally, each Council should have five rooms, one for use as a waiting room, one for the receptionist, and three for counselling. At present, only a minority of Councils have been able to achieve this, although standards are gradually improving throughout the country.

At the larger Marriage Guidance Councils there will be a permanent reception staff on duty at the premises during the day, but this will be the case at only twenty of the 122 Councils in the country. In the remainder of the Councils, reception duties are carried out by volunteers, or by the counsellors themselves. During the daytime it is particularly useful to have someone on the premises as well as the counsellor, because women clients tend to bring their small children with them and it is very difficult to do marriage counselling work effectively when the client's children are in the room. Several Marriage Guidance Councils keep a small stock of toys in the waiting room, and the receptionist will keep the children occupied while counselling goes on. In the evenings it is also most desirable to have someone to act as receptionist, particularly if the counsellor is a woman. All Marriage Guidance Councils try to recruit people in their own area to give practical help of this kind as receptionists, and it has been found that these receptionists sometimes decide to volunteer for counselling work.

A few Marriage Guidance Councils have installed a Post Office machine for answering the telephone when no one is manning the office. A message can be recorded on this machine, and this is played over to any client who telephones to make an appointment. The message asks the client to telephone again at a stated time when the office will be manned. Another Post Office service is operated for those appointments secretaries who operate from their homes. Under this scheme a 'ghost' telephone number is allotted to the Marriage Guidance Council; when this number is dialled the call is routed to the appointments secretary, although her own home telephone number is listed separately in the directory.

The administrative arrangements made for the clients are designed to make them feel accepted and understood, and to help create an atmosphere in which counsellor and client can talk to one another privately and without interruption. Clients know that they can return for further discussions if they wish, but that no pressure will be brought upon them to do this. Finally, they are assured that everything they say to the counsellor will be treated in absolute confidence.

Chapter 4

OTHER BRITISH SERVICES

This chapter deals with the marriage counselling and conciliation services operating in Britain, other than those of the National Marriage Guidance Council.

The Probation Service
The greatest volume of matrimonial conciliation work in Britain is being done by the Probation Service. About 43,000 cases are seen annually which involve marital problems, and in 26,000 of these cases some attempt at conciliation is being made. The Probation Service first developed, as have many of the modern social services in Britain, as a voluntary society. In 1872, the Church of England Temperance Society, which had been formed to prevent the drinking of alcohol, decided to expand its services. The first result of this decision was to start a service in the police courts, where men and women were being regularly convicted of petty offences, caused in the main by heavy drinking. The society appointed 'police court missionaries' to help these men to overcome drinking problems, and by the year 1900 there were over 100 of these missionaries, men and women, working voluntarily for the Temperance Society and attached to the various police courts.

From an early stage matrimonial conciliation work was done by these police court missionaries, because the marriages of the men and women they were helping were so often in difficulty, In addition, the police courts had been given power in 1895 to make matrimonial orders, so people with marriage problems came naturally to the courts where the missionaries were already working. At this stage the missionaries still considered themselves to be working for the Church of England and their work was supervised by a clergyman, but in 1907 the first major change in their status took place, following an Act of Parliament which made statutory provision for the appointment of probation officers whose salaries were to be paid out of public funds. The Act stated that the officers' task was to 'advise, assist and befriend' the people whom they were authorized to help, and this injunction still applies to the work that their successors are doing today. Many of the first officially appointed probation officers were the men and women who were already working as court missionaries.

The Service grew steadily and twenty years later, in 1926, male probation officers could expect to receive an annual salary of between £180 and £370; the scale for women officers varied from £150 to £270. These salaries were being paid partly out of local authority funds and partly by the government. At this time it was the general experience of probation officers that their matrimonial conciliation work was steadily growing, and this applied particularly to those officers who had become well known in their areas as being able to help with marriage problems. A government committee was set up in 1934 to consider all the work of the Probation Service, whose main function remained the supervision and rehabilitation of criminal offenders. The Committee's terms of reference included an instruction to enquire into 'the application of conciliation methods to matrimonial disputes, and the making of social investigations on behalf of the court'. When it reported, the Committee approved of the continuation of the matrimonial conciliation work of the probation officers and said that this work should be supervised in the same way as their other work. Officers were already responsible to probation committees made up of local magistrates, but from this time onward the Home Office took a larger part in their selection and training.

One result of the increasing influence of the Home Office in the selection and training of probation officers was a reduction in the numbers of those who were still working part-time, often carrying on with the job that they had begun some years before as court missionaries. Some of these part-time officers were being paid as little as £20 a year, mainly from private church funds. Following the Committee Report, however, all officers were to be paid and controlled by public authorities. At the present time, local authorities pay half the salary of officers working in their area and the government pays the rest, subject to a small deduction covering the cost of training, which is met by the local authorities themselves. The shift of emphasis from private to public control made it necessary for more attention to be given to the training of officers. Training was expected to include the general principles of social work, as well as a grounding in the law as it affected the work of the magistrates' courts, which had taken over the work of the old police courts.

In 1937 the existing marriage conciliation work of the officers was recognized by statute in the Summary Procedure (Domestic Proceedings) Act. During the Second World War, the few remaining officers who had not been called up for military service began to find that even more of their time was taken up in dealing with the marriage problems arising from the absence of so many men from their homes. When the war was over, the number of divorces rose very steeply, giving rise to an even greater need for conciliation work. The Denning Committee on Procedure in Matrimonial Causes, which reported in 1949 and which was responsible also for the first tangible recognition of the work of Marriage Guidance Councils, stressed the need for provision for the children of broken marriages. Probation officers were attached thereafter to the divorce courts to look into the welfare of children involved in divorce cases, and no divorce can now be granted unless the judge is satisfied that adequate arrangements have been made for the children of the marriage.

The training of probation officers had been first considered by a Government Committee in 1922, when it was suggested that the local committees responsible for the work of the officers should also see to their training. At this time, many of these committees represented the religious societies, and views on the most suitable type of training and experience differed widely. The whole matter of training came up again for consideration by the Committee set up in 1934. Its report recommended that a comprehensive training programme, supervised by a Central Training Board, should be instituted for probation officers. This Board was established and, although its activities were hampered during the war, it was able to provide a variety of forms of training for probation officers. By 1947, 350 out of 750 full-time probation officers had taken the training course provided by the Board. A few officers had taken social science courses at the universities, but these courses were not open to many officers because of the entrance qualifications demanded by the universities.

In the years since the war, the training of officers has received considerable attention and is now based on the most modern methods of casework. Prior to acceptance for training, officers have to undergo a form of selection which was first adopted, with the help of the National Institute for Industrial Psychology, in 1946. Home Office probation inspectors are responsible for the organization of the training courses, which involve a social science course leading to a diploma. After the diploma has been given there is a further year of training, most of which is undertaken in conjunction with practical work. The Probation Service has a training centre in London, where all aspects of officers' work are studied, including matrimonial conciliation.

During training, each of the new officers works with another more experienced officer who selects suitable cases for him or her to handle and supervises the work done. The officer in training has regular meetings with his senior colleague for discussion of the clients he is handling, and for this purpose he keeps regular case notes. Case discussions are also held where officers in training can gain from the experience of others. After a period of one year in training the officer will be interviewed by an inspector of the Probation Division of the Home Office. The inspector assesses his work and progress, in consultation with his senior colleagues, and under normal circumstances the local probation committee will then apply for confirmation of his position by the Probation Division.

Completion of training will not mean that there are no further opportunities for officers to improve their skills or their position in the Service. Many of them attend courses provided for the Probation Division by the Family Discussion Bureau, which operates in London as one of the activities of the Tavistock Institute of Human Relations, and whose matrimonial work is described later in this chapter.

The varying functions of the probation officer mean that he is well placed to help a considerable number of people with their marriage problems, often as a result of meeting them in connection with his court work. For example, an officer who is responsible for a boy who has been placed in his care on probation may find that some of the boy's difficulties stem from the stresses in the marriage of his parents, and he may be able to help with these. Against this advantage there is the undoubted association of the officer with the criminal courts, and this prevents some people from being willing to approach him for personal help. It is hard for officers to combine their legal functions, which are backed by the sanctions imposed by the law, with effective casework. Nevertheless, many of them succeed in doing this, in spite of heavy case-loads and rather inadequate offices.

The work-loads of probation officers are very high, one officer often handling as many as eighty or more cases at a time, many of which will involve conciliation work. One of the outstanding characteristics of marriage conciliation work is the amount of time it takes, and the heavy case-loads borne by most officers make it extremely hard for them to help all their clients as effectively as they would wish. This means that many officers give a great deal of their free time, especially in the evenings, helping people whom they cannot arrange to see during normal working hours. It is generally agreed that many of the offices used by officers are ill-equipped and inadequate. Interviews with clients have sometimes to take place in schools or in church halls, and this is not at all a helpful setting for an officer who is trying to persuade clients to relax and talk frankly about their problems. Such interviews normally only take place away from the main Probation Service centres but even these central offices are frequently unsuitable and cheerless. More attention needs to be given to the provision of wholly adequate premises for this work. The inadequacy of office accommodation often leads to the officers visiting the homes of the clients, though it seems generally agreed that this is by no means always likely to be helpful. It is not unusual for the officer to have to try to discuss the problems of husband and wife in a small room where the television set is still on. In spite of these difficulties it is abundantly clear that the conciliation work of the Probation Service steadily increases, and that its officers are able to turn adverse circumstances to good account.

The probation officer is not alone in the service he provides. His work is linked with that of the other local services, both statutory and voluntary. Contacts are maintained with the Child Care Service, the Family Service Units and also the Marriage Guidance Council. Referrals take place from one service to another, based on friendly contacts that have been established between the officers and the other social workers.

75

The conciliation work of the probation officer is confidential, but much of his other work is not so. For example, when dealing with a person placed on probation, it is his duty to make a report to the court when circumstances demand it. There must be occasions when it is hard for the officer to disentangle his legal duty to the court from the responsibility he owes to the client to respect his confidences. Nevertheless, this problem is solved by probation officers, who are fully accepted in the communities in which they work and who often receive calls from clients who were formerly on probation but who now visit them voluntarily when they need help. It has been decided[1] that statements made to an officer during an attempt at reconciliation are privileged communications, and if the parties object he cannot be made to disclose them in court. This is fully understood by magistrates, who do not expect officers to report on this aspect of their work, even when it is inextricably combined with their other functions.

The Family Discussion Bureau
The Family Discussion Bureau is the only specialized service in Great Britain offering help with marriage problems and using paid caseworkers. It was first set up in 1948 by the Family Welfare Association, an organization which continues to do marriage counselling work in the London area, but the bureau is now one of the five units of the Tavistock Institute of Human Relations. Almost all the caseworkers are employed on a part-time basis, and there are the equivalent of five workers available at the London centre, where the bureau sees its clients. The bureau does not confine its work to helping people with marriage problems; it also undertakes the training of caseworkers for other organizations, and research into the most effective training techniques of marriage counselling. The results of this research have been published from time to time.

The Tavistock Clinic, where the units of the Tavistock Institute operate, employs consultants, some of whom share in the work of the bureau, leading case discussions and supervising the work of the caseworkers. Normally, each client of the bureau sees a different caseworker, so that a husband and wife will

[1] McTaggart v. McTaggart (1948) 2 A11 E.R.754.

discuss their problems with a different person. Caseworkers also have regular discussions with one another. Clients are seen once a week for an hour. The caseworkers sometimes suggest a joint session at which both of them will be present, also the husband and wife. As is usual with a service of this kind, there is considerable pressure on the bureau, and clients often have to be asked to wait for an interview. It is sometimes possible for the bureau to offer a preliminary consultation before the clients come for regular interviews.

Although the supervisory staff are all medically qualified, the bureau is not operating as a part of the National Health Service. In spite of this, many clients are individually referred for help by practising doctors who are working within the Health Service. The clients of the bureau come from many walks of life, and about 130 new cases are seen each year. Only 29 per cent of these come direct to the bureau, the majority being referred by doctors and by social workers operating outside the Health Service. Clients are not asked to pay any fee for the help they receive.

The bureau trains its own workers, and since 1953 has also been training others as well. Four students a year are accepted for internal training, and they work at the bureau for three days each week. Residential courses which last three weeks and which are organized annually are provided for officers from the Probation Service, these courses being paid for by the Home Office. Many probation officers now doing marital reconciliation work have received their training from the Family Discussion Bureau. Training courses are also held for professional workers in other fields. These include doctors, lawyers, medical social workers, child care officers and others, and the cost of these courses is normally met by the authority that is employing the trainee, or occasionally by the trainee himself. One short series of lectures is also given at the London School of Economics, in addition to the regular participation by the staff in courses at universities and with professional bodies.

In recent years the bureau has received the greater part of its income from the Home Office by way of an exchequer grant, but it also receives grants from the Greater London Council. Grants have also been made by charities, in particular the Gulbenkian Foundation. The major part of this income is used in paying the salaries of the staff of the bureau, and only a small proportion is allotted for general administrative expenses.

The Catholic Marriage Advisory Council

The National Marriage Guidance Council had already been functioning for some years when, in 1945, the first steps were taken to establish a separate organization to help members of the Roman Catholic faith. The then Archbishop of Westminster, Cardinal Griffin, was particularly interested in sociology. He was approached by David Mace, then secretary of the National Marriage Guidance Council. David Mace had found that there were many problems then experienced by Roman Catholics that counsellors attached to the Marriage Guidance Councils were not qualified to handle, especially those relating to religious matters and to birth control. He suggested to the Cardinal that a Roman Catholic organization was needed, and in 1946 it was formed, being called the Catholic Marriage Advisory Council.

Cardinal Griffin had also been approached in 1945 by Mr Graham Green, a member of the Roman Catholic faith particularly interested in welfare work, with the suggestion that steps should be taken to help those members of their Church whose marriages were breaking down. The end of the Second World War was a time when the number of divorces was rising rapidly in Britain, and Cardinal Griffin asked Mr Green to undertake the formation of the new Council. It was incorporated in 1946 and obtained premises in Parliament Street, London, in September of that year. For the first five years of the life of the Council, the London centre was the only one in the country. In 1951 Mr Green retired from the work he had been doing, and Father Robert Gorman succeeded him. In the same year the first Catholic Advisory Centre outside London was set up, in Bristol, and this was followed in 1952 by the start of another centre in Liverpool, a city with a very large Roman Catholic population. Centres were set up in Oxford in 1953, in Blackpool, Lancaster, Preston and Ilford in 1954, and in another eight towns in the following two years. Thus by 1956 there were sixteen centres in operation.

Father Gorman was succeeded as chairman of the Council in 1956 by Father Maurice O'Leary, and under his leadership the number of centres has now grown to such an extent that there are seventy in operation. Two centres have been established in Scotland and five in Ireland, a country with a predominantly Roman Catholic population.

The Catholic Marriage Advisory Council bases its marriage counselling work on the use of very carefully selected and trained counsellors, all of whom have to be members of the Roman Catholic faith. The Council undertakes a considerable amount of educational work, and runs marriage preparation courses at its various centres. Help is also given to those members of the faith who wish to regulate the size of their families by methods that are acceptable to the Church. In 1966, some 309 medical advisers attached to the local centres were voluntarily giving their services in this particular sphere, and also in other ways. In the same year there were 418 trained counsellors at work.

The belief of the Church that marriage is indissoluble means that its members are less likely to resort to divorce, but this does not of course mean that Roman Catholics are immune from marriage difficulties. The Council believes, however, that members of their faith are more likely than most to take their marriage problems to a counsellor, because of their extreme reluctance to involve themselves in divorce proceedings. In 1966, some 10,241 families made use of the Council's facilities; this figure includes medical help as well as marriage counselling.

The counsellors help some clients in a way that is quite specific to their membership of the Roman Catholic faith. These clients have contracted marriages that may be invalid in the eyes of the Church, and it sometimes happens that the legal difficulties can be resolved with the help of the counsellors attached to the Council, and also of the legal advisers.

The Catholic Council shares with the National Marriage Guidance Council the view that an untrained and unsupported volunteer marriage counsellor, however well-intentioned, would be a danger to the clients he was trying to help. The Council uses as counsellors only married people with some years' experience of married life. Candidates are normally selected when aged between thirty and forty-five years. A university or professional background is the normal basic qualification for male counsellors. A similar background, though not necessarily the same qualifications, is required for women counsellors, many of whom have worked as doctors, nurses or social workers. It is not, however, the professional background that is the essential qualification; the selectors are looking for personal qualities that will enable the counsellors to help people with emotional as well as practical problems. The Council describes these qualities as the ability to listen and to inspire confidence, sympathy and yet objectivity of judgment, the true broadmindedness which enables an understanding of the difficulties of others, and a respect for the person and the personal responsibility of a fellow human being.

Selection conferences are held at weekends, and counsellors attend at the suggestion of the parish priest of their own local church. Unlike counsellors sponsored to work for the National Marriage Guidance Council, then, most Catholic counsellors come for selection at the direct suggestion of their own church. The selectors consist of an experienced counsellor, a priest and a psychiatrist. Rather less than half the candidates are selected. In 1966, 276 candidates were seen and 131 selected. Of 130 men, 54 (41·5 per cent) were successful, and of 146 women, 77 (52·7 per cent) were selected.

Following selection the counsellors are required to attend a training course that lasts eight months, involving attendance at weekends for a total of thirteen days. Counsellors study the principles and techniques of marriage counselling, the theology of marriage, civil and canon law, the psychology and physiology of marriage, and the social services available to the family. At the end of the training course, counsellors take an examination and if successful at this stage they are allowed to start work at a centre, initially on a probationary basis. Counsellors work with ecclesiastical, legal and medical advisers, all of whom give their services without payment. The counsellors normally bear their own expenses of travelling to and from the counselling centres.

Each centre has a priest as its chairman, and he is appointed by the Bishop of the Diocese who is in a position to act as spiritual consultant if required. The control of the Council's work remains therefore firmly in the hands of the clerical members of the church. Centres rely almost entirely on local diocesan organizations and members of the Catholic community. It is more difficult for Catholic centres to raise money from local authorities and from industrial concerns than for Marriage Guidance Councils, because of their denominational associations. The majority of centres are staffed by volunteers, but some of the larger ones are now employing paid staff. Where possible, the centres are set up in rooms separate from those used by other Roman Catholic organizations, where shy clients might worry about meeting people they know.

The Catholic Council receives a government grant of £8,000 a year towards the expenses of its work. Its headquarters are now at Clitherow House, 15 Lansdowne Road, London, and the majority of its income is used in selecting and training counsellors, paying staff salaries and generally administering the work of the Council. Income is also used in preparing and producing the various publications of the Council, and in circulating a regular bulletin.

A very large number of Roman Catholic organizations in other countries are now using the Catholic Marriage Advisory Council as their model in establishing similar centres in their own countries. The counsellors working in Eire and in the island of Malta have been trained by the British Council, and organizations are now developing in several countries in Latin America and in Mexico, following visits to those countries by the chairman of the Catholic Marriage Advisory Council in 1960.

The Scottish Marriage Guidance Council
The National Marriage Guidance Council works throughout England, Wales, Northern Ireland, the Channel Isles and the Isle of Man, but does not cover Scotland. The Scottish Marriage Guidance Council, with separate centres in thirteen Scottish towns, is operating a service on very much the same lines. Counsellors are selected and trained in a similar manner to counsellors working for Marriage Guidance Councils in the rest of Britain. The work of counsellors is regularly assessed by tutors who are paid a fee for this work. This assessment takes place during the probationary period that each counsellor has to serve following selection and training. The Scottish Marriage Guidance Council also provides in-service training for its counsellors through its salaried training officer, through psychiatrists and other paid tutors.

The Scottish Council was first formed in 1947, when local

Councils were established in Edinburgh and Glasgow. The main object of the Council was to establish new centres in other parts of Scotland, where it could be proved that these were necessary, and to undertake the selection, training and supervision of the counsellors. Most training has taken the form of weekly lectures and discussions held throughout the winter and spring months, but courses for some counsellors have been held residentially. The first National Conference of the Scottish Council was held in 1953, and this is now an annual event. On alternate years members of the public and other organizations are invited to attend. By the year 1967, counsellors attached to the thirteen Scottish Marriage Guidance Councils were giving 5,395 interviews annually to clients. This involved the handling of 1,939 cases and represented an increase on the figures for the previous year. This work was being undertaken by some 225 trained counsellors.

As is the case with the National Marriage Guidance Council, the work of the Scottish Council is financially supported by the government. The first grant from the Scottish Home and Health Department, amounting to £1,000, was made in 1956, and this grant has now been increased to £4,000 a year. Local authorities in Scotland also make grants towards the work of the Councils operating in their own areas. Apart from the annual exchequer grant of £4,000, the Scottish Council also receives approximately £500 a year from the local Marriage Guidance Councils. For the three years ending in 1967 an additional grant was given by the Carnegie Trust. This amounted to £2,000 a year and was given for the development of the basic training and in-service training of counsellors. The greater part of the Council's income is spent on the training programme, through staff salaries, fees for tutors and other items. Total expenditure is a little over £5,000 a year.

Steps were taken in Scotland by the government to consider the reorganization of the statutory social services, and the resulting proposals, known as the Kilbrandon Report, included the recommendation that the voluntary agencies already involved in social work should be encouraged to continue with this work and should receive appropriate government support. The Scottish Marriage Guidance Council has offered to continue with its work on the present basis, and has made a strong recommendation to the government that marriage counselling should not be attempted by anyone who has not had specific training for it. The Council has also stated that it might be able to develop its work in the direction of a family counselling service in a wider field than that of marital problems alone, and that a close working relationship between its own counsellors and social workers attached to the statutory services could be aided locally by the joint use of counselling rooms.

The Beth Din

The Beth Din is the Court of the Orthodox Jewish faith in Britain, and all its matrimonial proceedings require attempts at reconciliation to be made. Jewish religious law demands that every possible effort be made to reconcile husbands and wives whose marriages have broken down, and proceedings for a religious divorce coming before the Beth Din usually take place after a civil divorce has already been granted. The judge acts as conciliator, but it has been found by experience that this attempt at reconciliation is usually too late to be effective and a grant of divorce normally follows. Where no civil divorce has been granted but the parties are nevertheless proceeding for a divorce before the Beth Din, the judge is again expected to see them both in an attempt to reconcile them. He may also refer them to a Rabbi or to a member of the Jewish Marriage Education Council, but experience has again shown that by the time the husband or wife has petitioned for divorce there is very little hope of re-establishing the marriage.

If the attempts at reconciliation demanded by Jewish law prove fruitless, then a divorce will normally be granted on the grounds of mutual consent by both parties. In such circumstances it is expected that the husband shall initiate the legal proceedings before the Beth Din, and that the wife consent to the grant of the divorce. It is not possible for a wife to bring divorce proceedings before the Beth Din but, where a civil decree has already been pronounced, pressure is brought on the husband by other members of the Jewish faith to proceed with the divorce. Jewish law requires a husband whose wife has committed adultery to divorce her, and when this happens she is forbidden to marry the co-respondent.

As is the case in Britain generally and in many other parts of the world, it is not felt by those associated with the Beth Din courts that there is much hope of bringing about a reconciliation once the parties have fallen so far apart that they have actually commenced divorce proceedings. For this reason there is increasing emphasis among members of the Orthodox Jewish faith on the work of the Jewish Marriage Education Council, which is now concerning itself with marriage counselling as well as preparation for marriage. At the present time this Council is operating entirely privately and independently, and depends for its finances on Jewish men and women who support its work.

Chapter 5

AUSTRALIA

Marriage counselling in the Commonwealth of Australia is carried on by a variety of people and organizations, and the wide differences in the present patterns from State to State are an indication of the size of the country and the fact that each service has tended to develop on its own. Australia is a federation of States, and until 1959 there were different divorce laws in the States and territories that make up the Commonwealth. The Matrimonial Causes Act of 1959 provided one uniform divorce law for the whole country.

There are two main types of marriage counselling services in operation, the first concerning themselves specifically with marital problems and the second operating as part of a general family service. The first type of organization includes the Marriage Guidance Councils and other marriage guidance organizations approved of and supported by the Federal Government. Ten of these approved marriage guidance organizations are connected with the churches, and seven of the general family agencies have been similarly approved. An undefined amount of marital work is also done by probation officers, social workers, doctors, lawyers, clergy and others.

Although many of the Marriage Guidance Councils in Australia were first set up on the pattern of the similar Councils then operating in Britain, they have since developed in very different ways. In 1959, legislation was enacted by the Federal Government. The Matrimonial Causes Act of that year, which came into effect in 1961, gave power to the Commonwealth Government to make financial grants to approved marriage guidance organizations, and under the provisions of this Act the government is now subsidizing these organizations to the extent of some $213,350 a year. There are twenty such organizations receiving Federal support through the Attorney-General's Department in Canberra, the Federal Capital. In addition to this support from the Federal Government, seven of the approved organizations are also receiving grants from the State Governments.

The Attorney-General's Department is now supporting a nationwide marriage counselling service, using its power to recommend the payment of subsidies and thus to encourage the gradual improvement of this service. In 1960, the position of marriage guidance officer was created in the central office of the Attorney-General's Department in Canberra. Mr L. V. Harvey, a psychologist and a marriage guidance counsellor, was appointed to this position. The officer advises the government on the approval and the making of subsidies to organizations, and inspects the work of approved organizations. He acts therefore as a liaison between the government, which provides the funds, and the marriage guidance organizations which communicate their needs to the government and operate the counselling and conciliation services.

In the Marriage Guidance Councils the majority of the work with clients is carried out by volunteer counsellors, all of whom have been carefully selected and trained for their work, and who are regularly supervised by professionals. This, however, is not the universal pattern, for at some of the marriage counselling centres operated by Marriage Guidance Councils there are professional staff who have qualifications in psychology and social work. Equally, at the centres offering a general service to the family there are some counsellors who have not obtained a professional qualification and who are working as volunteers. These volunteers are subject to the supervision of the paid members of the staff. Again, and this illustrates the very diverse nature of the circumstances in which counselling work is done in Australia, a substantial number of the voluntary counsellors are themselves professional people who have qualifications in such different fields as medicine, law, education, theology, science, social work and psychology.

The Matrimonial Causes Act of 1959 made several other provisions in addition to those enabling the Federal Government to give grants in aid to marriage counselling agencies. Accredited marriage counsellors cannot be called to any court to give evidence of what has passed between them and their clients during marriage counselling interviews. Counsellors are required to take an oath of secrecy, and in return they receive this valuable privilege which protects them from being put under pressure by the lawyers of those clients who have decided to proceed for a divorce. The Act has also placed all solicitors under an obligation to inform their clients, when consulted about the possibility of a divorce, of the marriage counselling agencies available in their area. There is no obligation at that stage for the clients to attend for counselling. At present, 6 per cent of all clients coming to the Marriage Guidance Councils are referred from lawyers, and this proportion is tending to increase.

The judge hearing a divorce case is obliged by law to consider the prospects of reconciliation; he may adjourn the hearing of the divorce in order to enable one or both of the parties to see a conciliator, and even has the power to order them to do so. This power, however, is only exercised very rarely (fifteen referrals over a period of five years from 1961 to 1965), no doubt because an attempt at reconciliation under any form of duress is not likely to have much prospect of success. In addition, by the time the couple have reached the divorce court there is but little prospect that they will be willing to turn back, and for these reasons there is no disappointment in the Attorney-General's Department at the small number of occasions on which the judges have made referrals under the Act. The 1959 Act requires all marriage guidance organizations approved by the Attorney-General's Office to provide suitably qualified people to act as 'conciliators' when cases are referred by the court, and also requires those same organizations to give the Attorney-General details of the work done and the expense involved in providing their service. These organizations submit to the Attorney-General's Department an annual budget showing their anticipated expenditure during the coming year and also details, on a quarterly basis, of the counselling work in progress.

The marriage guidance officer of the Attorney-General's Department is regularly engaged in inspection and assessment of the work of Marriage Guidance Councils. In practice he finds that it is difficult to attend constantly to the needs of all Marriage Guidance Councils, and this results in particular attention being given to those who seem most in need of it or most able to use it. At the present time there are in each State Marriage Guidance organizations of a non-denominational character, and also the following other approved organizations:

the Church of England Marriage Guidance and Education Council in Melbourne; the Church of England Marriage Guidance Centre in Sydney; the Methodist Marriage Guidance Council, also in Sydney; the Catholic Marriage Advisory Council in Brisbane; the Catholic Marriage Guidance Council in Perth; the Catholic Welfare Organization in Canberra; and the sections devoted to marriage counselling work which are part of welfare organizations in the cities of Sydney, Melbourne and Adelaide.

Until recent years there had been very little attempt of the various different organizations to operate together, but in 1962 a Conference of Marriage Guidance Organizations (COMGO) was formed, consisting of representatives of all the organizations receiving grants. The initiative in calling the meeting that set up the conference was taken by the National Marriage Guidance Council of Australia, a body which until that time had acted mainly to collate information about the work of all the affiliated marriage guidance agencies. There have already been moves to share experience in the fields of selection and training, and inter-agency training sessions have been started. The fact that this conference has been so long in formation is at least partly due to the considerable distances that delegates have to travel; it costs over $300 to travel from Perth to Canberra. Among the members of the conference are the chairman of the National Marriage Guidance Council and the secretary of the Catholic Welfare Committees.

Grants to approved Marriage Guidance organizations since the passing of the Matrimonial Causes Act 1959 have risen from a total of $73,000 in 1960-1 to $213,350 in 1967-8. In the same period, the number of divorces in Australia rose from 6,709 in 1960 to 8,491 in 1965, and cases handled by the approved marriage guidance organizations from 4,854 in 1960-1 to 8,552 in 1965-6. It is now true to say that as many marriages are being handled annually by these organizations as are ending in divorce. There are 24 full-time and 26 part-time salaried workers at the approved organizations, in addition to the 356 volunteers. At some of the agencies a fee is charged to clients, though this is waived if the clients cannot afford it. Other efforts are made to raise funds from the public by way of subscription, and any individual helping the Marriage Guidance Councils in this way is allowed to deduct the donation from his income for tax purposes. Nevertheless, the main source of income of all the agencies is the Commonwealth Grant.

Attempts have been made to assess, so far as this is possible, the outcome of the counselling work. The figures given below reflect the impressions of the counsellors themselves, but it is interesting that they bear a close resemblance to similar figures produced in England and Wales.[1]

The figures for the period 1964-5 are as follow:

Problem apparently solved	13%
Relations improved, counselling concluded	18.5%
Relations improved, counselling continuing	13%
Referred for other help	9%
No improvement, but counselling continuing	7.5%

In the remaining 39 per cent of cases there appeared to have been no improvement at the time when counselling ended.

Other figures have been extracted for Australia as a whole from records submitted to the Attorney-General's office by the approved marriage guidance organizations. These indicate that, of some 28,662 interviews given to husbands and wives in 1965-6, some 14 per cent took place with both husband and wife present; 53 per cent of interviews were with wives and the remaining 33 per cent with husbands. Comparable figures for the National Marriage Guidance Council in Britain indicate rather different proportions; 5 per cent of interviews were with both husband and wife, 59 per cent with wives and 36 per cent with husbands. This reflects an increasing tendency in the Australian marriage guidance organizations to give joint interviews, a direct result of the influence of the Federal Government's marriage guidance officer who favours an interactional or family therapy approach, where appropriate.

It has already been mentioned that solicitors are obliged by law to mention to their clients the existence of marriage counselling agencies. The great majority of those coming to seek an interview with a counsellor (56 per cent) came on their own initiative; 18 per cent were referred by members of the clergy, 9 per cent by doctors and 3 per cent by other clients who had been to the counselling agencies.

[1] J. Wallis and H. S. Booker, Marriage Counselling, London, Routledge and Kegan Paul. 1958.

Another figure obtained from the Attorney-General's surveys shows that the average number of interviews for the year 1965-6 for each case handled by the organizations is 3·4. The comparable figure for 1961 was 2·8. There has been a steady rise in this average over the period, and as none of the clients were legally obliged to attend for counselling, this is considered to be an indication that the quality of the counselling work is improving. Since the year 1961 it is estimated that there has also been a 10 per cent rise in the proportion of cases who have had positive benefits from marriage counselling. Since 1965-6 the rise in the number of interviews per case has to some extent been offset by the increase in the number of joint interviews with husband and wife, but this practice is considered to give more rapid results and thus to reduce the number of interviews that are necessary.

The method of contact between the Attorney-General's Office and the marriage guidance organizations tends to vary from State to State and from organization to organization. In the larger organizations a director is employed, and dealings with the organization can quite simply be channelled through him. This is normally so with the Roman Catholic organizations, but in some cases it is necessary for the marriage guidance officer to negotiate with a committee, or even several committees. This very varied pattern is the inevitable result of making use of voluntary organizations dispersed over a wide area, and the marriage guidance officer is on record as saying that there is a need for maximum flexibility so as to avoid the kind of bureaucratic tendencies which may tend to de-humanize the relationship of a counselling agency with its clients. At the same time, there must be some degree of control and accountability, and some pattern of authority which makes certain that at least minimum standards are set and higher standards aimed at.[1]

At one time in the development of the marriage guidance officer's work it was suggested that he should provide a standard pattern for selection and training that should be mandatory for all marriage guidance agencies. This proposal was not put into effect, because an examination of the very differing organiza-

[1] L. V. Harvey, *The Federal Government and Voluntary Agencies working together in Marriage Guidance. Community Service.* F. W. Cheshire Ltd. Melbourne, 1966.

tions in Australia showed that one pattern would not suit them all. Moreover, if a pattern had been imposed it would have become necessary to inspect the organizations very regularly, and this was not possible. Instead, the marriage guidance officer has stated broad principles of selection and training, and it is left to the individuals running the organizations locally to apply them. The results are inspected by the officer, and after a visit he makes appropriate recommendations to the director of the organization or to its managing committee.

It is a fundamental principle of voluntary counselling in Australia that the counsellors should be closely supervised. The tendency is for this supervision to be more frequent in the early stages of training than later on, and new counsellors may well spend as much time being supervised as they do in counselling. Supervision is usually carried out by a professionally qualified person working voluntarily, but it may also be done by a salaried member of the marriage guidance organization staff, assuming that he has the appropriate qualifications. In addition to the voluntary work of qualified people in supervising the work of the counsellors, there is also a great deal of voluntary work done by professionals in the process of the selection and training of counsellors.

During the early stages of the development of the marriage guidance services in Australia, as in Britain, there was considerable professional scepticism of the value of the work that could be done by volunteers, and the motives of those who wanted to undertake marriage counselling were called in question. Gradually, an increasing number of professional people became convinced that the counsellors were able to do a worthwhile job. There are not in fact enough professional workers to meet the needs of married people with problems, and if it were not for the volunteer workers it would be impossible to provide the service at all.

In each local organization there is a considerable amount of work to be done to enable the counsellor's task to be carried on effectively and smoothly. Appointments have to be arranged for clients and counsellors, meetings of counsellors and supervisors fixed, committee meetings organized, correspondence answered. All this work is done by the office staff, normally under the supervision of the director.

There are undoubtedly difficulties as well as advantages in the use of volunteer workers. One major problem is to ensure that counsellors do sufficient work to enable their standards to be maintained. One cannot ask too much of a volunteer, especially when, in addition to the counselling, he is expected to keep case notes, attend case discussions and do a good deal of travelling. Nevertheless, regular experience is essential if the work is to be effective, and in Australia a minimum of three hours' counselling is expected of all counsellors each week. Many do more than this. Some counsellors withdraw temporarily from the work owing to illness, moving house, pregnancy or other causes. If a counsellor ceases counselling work for more than a few weeks he can only resume subject to special conditions. These usually involve extra supervision or additional training. Additionally, a number of women counsellors, seeking an additional source of income, give up counselling for other work, or seek to take up similar work on a professional basis, after additional training. Several counsellors now working in Australia are also taking degree courses at universities, their ultimate intention being to take up professional social work, at which time they will cease to work as volunteers for the marriage guidance agencies.

The Australian National Marriage Guidance Council was formed in 1952, and represents the constituent State Councils. Its income is entirely derived from them, and its meetings are attended by one representative of each of the State Councils, with the Marriage Guidance Officer from the Attorney-General's Department also in attendance. The National Council's main concern has been with practical developments in marriage guidance work in the Commonwealth. It forms a loose but valuable co-ordinating link between the State Councils whose work represents the real strength of the marriage guidance movement in Australia, and it has created the Conference of Marriage Guidance Organizations already referred to.

Marriage Guidance Council of New South Wales
Sydney is the State Capital of New South Wales, where the Marriage Guidance Council has established four counselling centres. There is also a centre at Newcastle on the coast some eighty miles north of Sydney, and steps have been taken to set

up provisional committees in the towns of Tamoorth and Armidale, both of which are inland and to the north of Newcastle, and in Wollongong, south of Sydney. One of the centres recently set up in Sydney was financed for its first year entirely by the local Rotary club, which raised enough money to equip its premises and to pay rent and other expenses. In Sydney there are about 3,000 interviews given yearly to clients, and about 500 and 200 interviews respectively in Newcastle and Wollongong. Sydney is using seventeen trained counsellors, some of whom are paid a fee; Newcastle has nine counsellors and Wollongong two. The main Sydney centre has five counselling rooms and a large general office, and is situated over a large department store. There is a director, a secretary and several other office workers.

The major expenses of the Marriage Guidance Council are salaries of around $15,000 and rent of about half that sum. Money is also spent on extension work. Income is mainly derived from the Federal Government, but a small grant is also received from the State Government. There are also various donations from individuals and from firms.

New South Wales is the State in which there are the largest number of different approved marriage counselling organizations for, in addition to the Marriage Guidance Council, there are also Church of England, Methodist and Roman Catholic organizations, a professional Social Welfare Organization and the Father and Son Movement. The organizations other than the Marriage Guidance Council now share the same counsellor selection and training programme, and it is of some interest that the Marriage Guidance Council of New South Wales is not included in this joint programme.

Queensland Marriage Guidance Council

The headquarters of this Council are in a converted bungalow in Brisbane. There is a full-time director who is a qualified psychologist, and also an honorary secretary, as well as the usual office staff. There is a full-time salaried chief counsellor at the centre who also acts as head of the selection and training programme. There are also centres of the Queensland Marriage Guidance Council at Toowoomba, west of Brisbane, and at Rockhampton and Townsville which are respectively 450 and

850 miles north of Brisbane. These centres are visited regularly by the director. This Council started a publication entitled *Marriage* which has now been taken over by the National Marriage Guidance Council of Australia.

South Australia Marriage Guidance Council
This Marriage Guidance Council developed from a standing committee of the South Australian Council of Social Services, which in 1947 was asked to act as a marriage guidance committee. The first State grant was made in 1951, and in 1954 this was raised sufficiently to enable the Council to open its own centre in Adelaide. There is also now a centre in Elizabeth. The Adelaide Centre employs a director of counselling and also a director of family life education, both of whom are paid a salary. There are some twenty-four active counsellors, and interviews are given by appointment on weekdays. Most clients make their appointments by telephone, and there is only a short waiting list. A recent attempt to recruit more counsellors was not very successful, and from a total of only twelve applications a training course for eight counsellors was started. The number of clients tends to rise only slowly, there being 1,789 interviews in 1966.

The average age of the partners in the marriages helped seems substantially lower than in Britain. In about half the cases seen in a recent year (221 out of 514) the wife was aged between 20 and 24 years; in another 131 cases the wife was aged between 25 and 29. This means that in over 68 per cent of the cases helped by the Marriage Guidance Council the wife was aged under 30. There are other emphases on youth in the work of this Council, which is pursuing a considerable family life education programme.

The Council has obtained good local publicity through *The Advertiser*, a newspaper circulating in Adelaide, which runs a weekly feature known as 'Family Forum'. Counsellors attached to the Council give their views on various problems affecting family life, and the paper makes substantial payments to the Council, which as a result is not short of funds. Another attempt to secure public interest is through the recruitment of subscribing members of the Council, each of whom is expected to pay at least $1 a year. If they pay $4 they receive copies of the journal *Marriage Guidance* published in England by the National Marriage Guidance Council, an indication of the continuing maintenance of contacts between Australia and Britain.

Tasmania Marriage Guidance Council

This Marriage Guidance Council has two main centres, in Hobart and Launceston. At one stage these centres were run quite separately, but money available from the government has enabled the appointment of a director of the Council, and the work of the Hobart and Launceston centres has been brought closer together. Geographically, they are over 100 miles apart, and both have their own premises. At the Launceston branch some five counsellors handle rather over sixty cases a year, and the scale of operations of this Council is less than that of the Marriage Guidance Councils on the mainland of Australia.

Victoria Marriage Guidance Council

There are four organizations in Melbourne, Victoria, offering a marriage counselling service and approved by the Federal Government. The Marriage Guidance Council has only recently acquired new premises which cost over $30,000, and obtained a large proportion of this money on loan. The mortgage repayments and interest are no more than the annual rental payments on the former premises used by the Council. The seventy counsellors working in the main centre are giving about 4,000 interviews a year. Counselling also is given at Geelong, Latrobe Valley and at Warrnambool in the State of Victoria, but the great majority of clients live in the Melbourne area. There are five counsellors working at Geelong, and eight at Latrobe Valley.

The Marriage Guidance Council has appointed a selection board and a training board, and the senior counsellors act as supervisors of their less experienced colleagues; twenty senior counsellors are in this way supervising the work of fifty others, being themselves supervised by professional members of the Council. The Council has appointed a director, at present the Reverend L. Phillips, who is also secretary of the National Marriage Guidance Council of Australia.

The other approved organizations in Victoria are the Church of England Marriage Guidance and Education Council, the Catholic Family Welfare Bureau and the Citizens Welfare

Service of Victoria. There are close links between the Victoria Council and the Church of England Council, the counsellors of each organization having their training together; there has not, however, been any formal merger of the two organizations, possibly because the Church body was established first and wishes to maintain its independence.

Western Australia Marriage Guidance Council

Western Australia is separated from the other States by the desert that occupies the greater part of the centre of the country. Its capital, Perth, is some 1,500 miles from Adelaide in South Australia and about 2,000 miles from Sydney on the eastern seaboard. This great distance has its effect on communications between Eastern and Western Australia, and on the development of social services. The Commonwealth Government gives the Western Australia Marriage Guidance Council a grant of $14,000 a year, and the State Government $7,000 a year. The State grant is rather higher in proportion to that given by most of the other States, an indication of the independent nature both of the State and of its Marriage Guidance Council.

The Marriage Guidance Council is active and has recently appointed its own full-time director of counselling services, who is a clinical psychologist. All counsellors have to take an eighteen months' training programme consisting of two hours' work each week. Selection takes place at the end of the training course, although there is also a substantial degree of selection at the initial stage as well, only fourteen out of fifty candidates having been accepted for a recent training course. Counsellors are expected to give between three and five hours of their time each week to counselling, and the thirty-one active counsellors in 1967 gave 3,070 interviews in the year. The average number of interviews for each case, not inclusive of the 'intake' interview, is 9·01. In addition to the Perth centre, the Marriage Guidance Council offers counselling at Bunbury and Kalgoorlie, and plans also to extend the service to Geraldton, which is about 250 miles north of Perth. The Perth centre is well equipped and contains six counselling rooms. There are several staff members assisting the director, and the major part of the Council's income is used in paying salaries. Other expenses include the National Marriage Guidance Council levy, the cost of travelling by counsellors and by others, and the expenses of running the counselling centres.

A particular feature of the Western Australia counselling service is the intake interview, normally lasting about ten to fifteen minutes. This interview was instituted by the director, who normally conducts the interview himself and who allocates the client to one of the counselling team. The counsellor will normally see the client within two or three days. The Council feels that this intake interview by a professional psychologist enables the counsellors to obtain considerable help from the director, who will himself have seen the client. Another unusual feature of this service is that each counsellor is accompanied at his first interviews with a client by a more experienced counsellor, whose function is to observe and later to guide the new counsellor in his methods of work. It is apparently only rarely that the clients object to seeing more than one counsellor, but this practice is not in use in other parts of Australia, or in Great Britain. All counsellors attached to the Council are authorized to continue work on an annual basis, the decision on re-authorization being made by the director of counselling services.

Canberra Marriage Guidance Council

This Council was established in the early 1960s by a group of clergy and interested laymen, and by 1965 it had reached a standard which enabled it to be approved by the Attorney-General as a marriage guidance organization. Shortly afterwards it was admitted as an affiliated member of the National Marriage Guidance Council and also became a member of the Conference of Marriage Guidance Organizations. It is now operating from premises in Canberra consisting of two rooms, and deals with over seventy cases a year, involving almost 300 interviews. Some fourteen volunteer counsellors work for the Marriage Guidance Council, and more are being trained to meet the needs of the most rapidly growing city in Australia.

Chapter 6

NEW ZEALAND

The National Marriage Guidance Council of New Zealand is an autonomous body, closely linked to the Department of Justice. There are twenty-one affiliated Marriage Guidance Councils in different parts of the country, using the services of forty-nine accredited counsellors, and a further fifty-six counsellors are in various stages of training. The counsellors are supervised by over eighty tutors, most of whom have professional qualifications in psychiatry or social work but who give their services without charge. The first steps to set up a marriage counselling service were taken in New Zealand in 1947, and in 1948 a Marriage Guidance Council was established in Christchurch. The preparatory steps had been taken by the local Junior Chamber of Commerce, who had convened a meeting to discuss the need for family life education. Representatives from the churches and from community organizations attended, and from these discussions emerged a decision to investigate the marriage counselling work then going on in Britain. The New Zealand National Council of Churches made contact with the Reverend E. P. Blamires, who was in England at that time, and he studied the work of the National Marriage Guidance Council then operating in London, reporting his conclusions to the Council of Churches. A Marriage Guidance Council was then formed on lines similar to the British Council.

When Mr Blamires returned from England a 'home and family week' was organized in New Zealand, and this brought a good deal of publicity for the new Marriage Guidance Council. A second Council was started in Dunedin, and others began to form themselves. The good intentions of the founders in some parts of the country did not always come to fruition, and many of these early Councils dissolved almost as quickly as they had formed, there being very little public support and no help from the government. It was not possible to make much progress during the next decade, but in 1959 the secretary of justice, head of the Department of Justice, decided that a worthwhile service was not likely to come into being without government support. The Department was already closely involved with social problems having their roots in marriage breakdown, and decided to take the first steps to promote marriage counselling on a national basis.

The Department of Justice appointed an adviser on marriage guidance, and in 1960 a conference of interested parties was held. Its recommendation, accepted by the Minister of Justice, was that an advisory committee on marriage guidance be appointed. The committee represented the three government departments concerned with justice, education and health. There were also members from the then existing Marriage Guidance Councils, the National Council of Churches, the Roman Catholic Church and the University of Wellington. The function of the committee was to advise the Minister of Justice through his secretary; decisions on policy would be taken by the Minister.

It was decided at the outset to try to create an autonomous organization which could operate with government support but which would not be a state service. The first practical step was to provide for the selection and training of counsellors, the money for this programme being provided by the government. In the comparatively short space of seven years considerable progress was made, with the result that well over one hundred counsellors are now working in different parts of New Zealand. The sponsoring of candidates for selection and training is in the hands of the twenty-one local Marriage Guidance Councils and of such other organizations as can meet the established requirements relating to work and supervision. There is no division of counselling services between the churches, as is sometimes the case in Australia, so the selectors are concerned only with the suitability of candidates for counselling work, and not with their religious beliefs.

A pilot scheme was decided upon, and a Marriage Guidance Council was set up near Wellington, on the North Island. It was entirely financed by the government, which provided the necessary rooms, equipment, and the services of a receptionist. This particular Marriage Guidance Council has gradually begun to take over responsibility for raising some part of its own income, and is able to make small annual repayments to the

Treasury. The government has already appointed the adviser on marriage guidance, and later provided for the engagement of a regional adviser, whose function is to supervise the development of marriage counselling in the province of Auckland. A director of counselling services for Auckland was appointed in 1968 on a part-time basis at an annual salary of $2,000.

The National Marriage Guidance Council of New Zealand, which represents the affiliated Councils, elects an executive to manage the affairs of the organization. Its secretary receives an honorarium, and there are committees established to review policy on marriage counselling and on family life education work. Annual conferences are held at which members from all areas attend.

The Domestic Proceedings Act of 1939 had made provision for conciliation in respect of applications made to magistrates' courts for separation or maintenance orders, and other types of order. Orders of this type can be sought on allegations of cruelty, drunkenness or assault. Before any complaint reaches the stage of being set down for a court hearing it is referred by the magistrate to a conciliator appointed by him, the conciliator being required to interview the parties with a view to effecting a reconciliation. Nothing said by the parties to the conciliator can be received in evidence in any later proceedings in court.

It is open to the magistrate to dispense with the conciliation procedure and this was frequently done, simply because there were not enough people suitable for this work. In recent years, however, the courts have begun to turn to the trained marriage counsellors working for the Marriage Guidance Councils. In cases where volunteer counsellors are concerned, the New Zealand Department of Justice makes a direct payment for their conciliation services to the Marriage Guidance Council to which they are attached.

In one recent year, marriage counsellors working as conciliators for the magistrates' courts in Auckland and Otahuhu had 363 cases referred to them. About 13 per cent of these cases never came to the counsellors for help, some telephoning to say that they had reconciled, others that they had finally parted. Of the 314 cases seen, reconciliations were reported in sixty-one cases. Counsellors reported that in one third of the cases referred the wife had either had a child before the marriage took place, or was pregnant at the time of the marriage. They also reported that there seemed to be a marked degree of mental instability in about a quarter of the cases seen.

In addition to the conciliation provisions in the 1939 Act, there has now been passed into law the Matrimonial Proceedings Act 1963, which makes similar provisions for consideration of the prospects of reconciliation in divorce cases. Section 4(b) of the Act reads (*inter alia*) that:

'If at any time it shall appear to the Court . . . that there is a reasonable prospect of reconciliation, the Court may adjourn the proceedings to afford those parties an opportunity to become reconciled, or may nominate a suitable person with experience or training in marriage counselling, or in special circumstances some other person, to endeavour, with the consent of those parties, to effect a reconciliation.'

The Act also provides for all statements made to a counsellor to be absolutely privileged. Although some referrals to counsellors have been made under the provisions of this legislation, it is too early to say whether they are proving effective.

Counsellors working for the Marriage Guidance Councils in New Zealand are recruited by friends and acquaintances already associated with the Councils, by appeals to clubs and church groups, and by letters to the press and advertisements. Candidates then have to go through a sponsoring procedure, the local Marriage Guidance Council arranging interviews by three or four people. Sponsoring forms and references are completed and sent to the National Marriage Guidance Council, which calls candidates to the selection and training centre established at a residential Training Centre in Wellington. The selection weekend, which lasts from Friday to Sunday, is organized by the advisory committee of the Justice Department, and the Department provides all travel expenses, by air where necessary, and also meets the cost of accommodation. Candidates are notified of the results of the selection conference by telegram on the day following the selection weekend.

Successful candidates are expected to attend four weekend courses at the training centre during the first year, and their training includes counselling work under supervision. The first two weekends are separated by an interval of between four and six weeks, after which counsellors begin work. After another period of two months the third training course is held, when counsellors can bring their preliminary experiences of counselling for discussion and guidance. The last training weekend follows about a year after the original date of selection, and counsellors remain together throughout their training programme. Local professional supervision of counsellors is done on a weekly basis, and counsellors are also expected to attend case discussions at least once a month.

The training programme covers all aspects of the work that the counsellors are likely to meet, and each training weekend consists of nine instructional periods of one and a half hours each. In addition to a consideration of the principles of counselling and the development of the human personality, attention is given to the medical, spiritual and legal aspects of counselling. Tape recorders and films are also used, and pre-marital counselling is discussed.

Approximately two years after the original selection of a counsellor he can expect to become officially accredited by the National Marriage Guidance Council. For this purpose the supervisor submits a report on the work of the counsellor on a special form. This is sent to the advisory committee office, and deals with the number of cases handled, the special weaknesses and strengths of the counsellor, and details of any difficulties which have been overcome. The supervisor is asked to assess whether the counsellor can now be regarded as ready to continue with the work with or without supervision, or possibly with reduced supervision. At the same time as this report is received from the supervisor, the Justice Department also receives a report from the Marriage Guidance Council to which the counsellor is attached. This indicates the way in which the counsellor has co-operated with the Council, attended case discussions, and been available on a regular basis for counselling work. When a counsellor is formally accredited he is then invited to a graduation dinner attended by representatives of the government, including the Minister of Justice, who gives each successful graduate a letter of accreditation.

Following accreditation the counsellor can expect to receive supervision on a reduced basis, and is required to be re-accredited each year. Re-accreditation reports are submitted in similar form to those already described for first accreditation. A close watch is kept on the amount of work done by counsellors, it being considered that a basic minimum is necessary in order to maintain standards. Counsellors in training are expected to have only one or two interviews each week during the first year, but experienced counsellors will normally give a maximum of four weekly interviews. Allowance is made for one month's holiday a year, and appropriate provisions are made to enable clients to receive support while their counsellor is on holiday. All these rules and procedures are laid down in the *Handbook* which gives a guide for counsellors and is produced by the National Marriage Guidance Council.

The *Handbook* describes the appropriate provision for reception duties at counselling centres. It is expected that receptionists be employed to arrange appointments by telephone, and to have available lists of related agencies. Names and addresses of counsellors, clients and of committee members are kept. Donations have to be collected and publications sold, and in a large and busy marriage guidance centre these duties demand the services of a full-time employee.

It is also a matter of policy for the National Council to provide chaperonage for counsellors whenever the receptionist is absent, or when there is no other counsellor working at the marriage guidance centre. A chaperone is always required when the counsellor is seeing a client of the opposite sex, and when the client requests a chaperone. It is left to the counsellor to make the arrangements for a chaperone to attend. It is only on rare occasions that difficulties have been known to arise, but similar provisions exist in Great Britain, where the National Marriage Guidance Council especially encourages its member Councils to provide chaperonage, especially when counsellors are working during the evenings.

As is normal in other parts of the world, counsellors keep detailed case notes and records of their work, and these notes are available for scrutiny by the supervisors. When a client is enrolled at a first interview it is the duty of the receptionist to provide the counsellor with an envelope which contains a front sheet designed to give factual details about the client, and also case note sheets. Each case is allotted a number for reference purposes, and record sheets and case notes are kept in envelopes in locked filing cabinets. The *Handbook* gives details of the main elements that counsellors are expected to record in their case notes. The annual records of the work of all Marriage Guidance Councils are extracted from these case records.

An unusual procedure in New Zealand is the occasional use of a tape recorder during counselling interviews. The aim of this is to aid the counsellor in learning about the work that he is doing. The National Marriage Guidance Council has laid down some rules for the use of tape recorders in these circumstances, the first being that the recorder and its microphone must be prominently displayed in the interview room. The consent of the client must also be obtained, and he must be told that he is free to turn the recorder off at any moment if he wishes to do so. It is normal for the client's consent to the use of a recorder to be obtained in writing, and he must always be told the purpose for which it is being made. This purpose may be to enable the counsellor to review his interviewing technique, and to understand and help his client more effectively; it may also be used to enable the counsellor and his supervisor to understand the case. In some instances these tapes are used for the training of counsellors, in which case any names mentioned on the tapes are erased in order to preserve anonymity. Finally, tapes can be used as the basis for publications.

One would expect many clients to have substantial reservations about the use of tape recorders in this way, and there seems to be some danger that clients might agree to their use, not so much because they really wanted to do so, but because they do not wish to offend the counsellor who has been helping them. As a reassurance, it is obligatory for counsellors using recorders to inform clients that the tape will be stored in a locked cabinet at the counselling centre, and that it will be erased when it is no longer required. Counsellors have to be familiar with the workings of recorders, and to be completely at ease in front of a microphone.

The major source of revenue of the National Marriage Guidance Council of New Zealand, and of its constituent Councils, is the Golden Kiwi grant. The Golden Kiwi Board of Control administers a national lottery, some of the proceeds of which are diverted to the National Council. There are six members of the Board of Control, and they include the Prime Minister, the Leader of the Opposition, and the Minister of Internal Affairs who acts as chairman. There are several committees responsible for administering different aspects of the board's work, and it is the welfare services distribution committee that determines the grant paid to the National Marriage Guidance Council. The Secretary for Justice is a member of this committee. The annual income of the board is approximately £1,000,000, and the welfare services distribution committee deals with the allocation of about £215,000 out of this sum. Lotteries are held in New Zealand about sixty or seventy times a year, tickets normally costing five shillings. In the years from 1964 to 1967 the annual grant paid to the Council from the Golden Kiwi fund rose from £14,600 to £17,500. This increase has been made necessary by the growth in the number of centres, it being estimated that a large counselling centre costs about £1,000 a year to run. Although the costs of providing the service continue to rise, it has not been possible for the Marriage Guidance Councils to obtain substantial increases in Golden Kiwi grants, because the income of the fund is not tending to rise from year to year.

Because of the unlikelihood of further increases in the grants from the Golden Kiwi Board, local Marriage Guidance Councils have increasingly been forced to attempt to raise funds on their own account. The aim is normally to raise 17 per cent of their annual budgets in their fourth year of operation, 20 per cent in their fifth year and 25 per cent in their sixth year. A few, notably the centre at Wellington, are able to raise a higher proportion than this. The National Marriage Guidance Council makes a report each year to the Golden Kiwi Board of Control, and has been able to point to the fact that the divorce rate in New Zealand in relation to the number of new marriages has been steadily dropping, from 10 per cent in 1963 to 8.3 per cent in 1965.

The National Marriage Guidance Council is on record as saying that the time may come when the Government of New Zealand may have to take over full financial responsibility for the marriage guidance service. It was through the good offices of the government that the grants from the Golden Kiwi Board were first obtained, but many people associated with the work of the Councils have reservations about the continuance of this form of support, some because it cannot be guaranteed as a permanency, others on the grounds that the money has been raised by means of a lottery, a process to which they have personal objections.

The ultimate need for a national headquarters for the National Marriage Guidance Council in New Zealand is recognized, but it is accepted that at the present time this aim is not capable of fulfilment. Nevertheless, in a comparatively short time it has been possible to develop a comprehensive marriage counselling service, staffed by skilled volunteers closely supervised by professionals, many of whom give their services without fee. It can reasonably be said that the close association of the government with the Council's work has proved to be a success, and that this association has not in any way restricted the freedom of the Council to develop on its own lines.

Chapter 7

SCANDINAVIA AND FINLAND

Norway

In Norway, it is not particularly difficult to obtain a divorce, but the law provides that some attempt at reconciliation must be made. Most divorces follow a period of agreed separation, and only a small percentage are granted on the grounds of infidelity or cruelty. If one partner deserts the other, a divorce can take place at the request of either party after a period of three years.

Before a divorce can be granted by the court, the person seeking the divorce must have attempted reconciliation either through a minister of religion or through one of the members of a local reconciliation board. These members are elected by the people, and are not paid for their work, and the partner seeking the divorce has the choice of visiting one of them, or a pastor. In fact, this is something of a formality, and a recent survey showed that the average time taken for each reconciliation interview with a member of the reconciliation board was only ten minutes.

There are several family counselling organizations in Norway, and it is open to any of them to apply to the government to be recognized as having the right to undertake this form of legal reconciliation work. By no means all of them have done this, and indeed some of them prefer not to do so. The organizations that do will normally issue a certificate at the end of the counselling interviews stating, if this is the case, that counselling has been attempted but without positive result. A rather similar certificate is issued by the pastor or member of the reconciliation board when the parties have been to see him.

It often happens that the members of the reconciliation boards (which exist to assist the negotiated settlement of other legal claims as well as matrimonial disputes) refer the parties to the family counselling centres. The first family counselling centre in Norway was started by the Mothers' Hygiene Bureau in Oslo. The major function of this bureau was, and is still, to offer help and guidance to women who are applying for a legal abortion.

In the course of this work the bureau frequently met women whose marriages were in difficulty, and so they extended the abortion service to covering marriage counselling, using a psychiatrist and paid social workers. The bureau was originally privately financed, but since 1959 it has been wholly paid for and run by the state, although the people in charge remain the same. The work continues to expand, but a visitor gains the impression that most family problems are considered to have a medical basis and are usually treated by medically trained workers. All workers at the bureau, for instance, wear long white coats, and the atmosphere is rather that of a clinic than of a counselling centre.

The development of family counselling centres has been, to quote Magne Langholm, 'scattered and haphazard, and practically confined to the major towns'.[1] There are three main types of family counselling centre, all of which provide a service of support for the whole family. In some of the smaller towns the centres are staffed by trained social workers who are paid for their work, and it seems that the standard of counselling varies considerably from place to place, depending on the skill of the individual worker.

The Health Ministry also set up medical family counselling centres in two northern areas of the country, on an experimental basis, and the number of these centres is now being expanded. Each centre is under the direction of a psychiatrist, and is staffed by social workers and also sometimes by nurses and midwives. It is financed by the government. There is naturally a strong medical bias to the work, and these centres undertake a lot of family planning and child care work in addition to the counselling service which they make available to all members of the family. There is, in fact, no particular concentration on marriage counselling as such. In the medical family counselling centres in Oslo there is always a full-time psychiatrist as well as a psychologist at work.

One such centre is under the direction of a psychiatrist; he is assisted by a psychologist and by two social workers, and he aims to expand the centre by employing an increasing number of social workers to deal with family problems. This would improve the amount of counselling support for clients referred to the

[1] *Family and Child Welfare in Norway.* Magne Langholm. 1961.

centre, given by social workers under his supervision. At this centre it is quite normal for the whole family, including the children, to be seen together, and marriage counselling is thought of as only a part of a comprehensive family service.

Some clients come direct to this centre, and some are referred for help. Members of the reconciliation boards have made some referrals, but the centre finds these clients difficult to help, as they have often come only because they feel they are legally obliged to do so. Here, as in many other countries, compulsory conciliation is not considered to be of any value in preventing divorce or marriage breakdown. Nevertheless, a good deal of supportive work is done by the centre in cases where a divorce cannot be avoided, but where it is often possible to make life more tolerable for both partners and for any children of the marriage. Clients seen at the centre are from all social categories, and are not asked for any fee. The service is financed entirely by the Oslo Board of Health. As this centre has the advantage of supervision by the psychiatrist and support from the psychologist and social workers, it is possible to place a good deal of emphasis on helping married couples to communicate with one another more effectively. The psychiatrist in charge of the centre considers that this is more helpful to clients than the less active role of the counsellor, who is concerned mainly to help his clients express their feelings rather than to aim at producing any particular change in the relationship between husband and wife. All workers at the centre join in at least two case discussions each week, led by the psychiatrist.

The third main type of family counselling centres in Norway are those run by the churches. The largest of these operates in Oslo, and has grown steadily since its foundation in 1939. Originally the work of helping people with family problems was done by doctors and pastors, and the centre published a small number of booklets on sexual matters. They received some letters and visits from clients, and in 1952 established a centre in Oslo where counselling could be given on a regular basis. This was extended in 1957, and a part-time social worker was employed, working full-time in the following year. By 1967 the centre was using the services of six people, all of whom received a salary. A psychiatrist and a psychologist are paid for part-time services, and apart from the office staff there are three trained social workers, the leader of whom is also the director of the centre. This is a typical pattern for a family counselling centre, where very little voluntary work is done. In some country districts there is a certain amount of voluntary work by doctors and other professional people, but no lay counsellors are used either at the Church Family Counselling Centre or at any other centres in Norway.

The Church Centre in Oslo is mainly financed by the city of Oslo and by the Public Health Insurance Scheme, but about one third of its income is derived from church sources. The government has recently decided to make a total grant of £2,500 to aid all the church centres in the country, and the Oslo centre will use only £350 of this sum. The centre is recognized by the State as eligible to receive grants from the Public Health Insurance Scheme, and money received from this source currently amounts to about £2,000 a year. Eligibility follows from the employment of the psychiatrist, and payments are made to the centre in relaton to the amount of work done, and on the basis that the client's problem has some medical content. To qualify for a grant the difficulty in the family has to have caused or threatened illness, imposed serious stress on the client, or caused his work to suffer. When these conditions apply, the public health insurance pays 100 *krone* (about £5) for a short-term contact involving three hours' work and 360 *krone* (about £18) for a long-term contact, involving twelve hours' work. There is also provision for further payments to cover extended counselling at the rate of 30 *krone* per hour.

Although the centre is responsible to a diocesan board, there is in fact no religious teaching involved in the counselling work, and the centre is run in the same way as any other counselling centre. Clients are seen by appointment, at the centre, usually as the result of a telephone call. No client is asked for a fee, although a few make contributions towards the expenses of the work. In about 80 per cent of the cases the social worker sees both husband and wife, and occasionally the marital home is visited. However, visits of this kind are rare and normally occur only when the centre is exercising a medical responsibility, such as a recommendation relating to a legal abortion. Understandably, most applications for abortions tend to go to one of the other family counselling centres, and not to the church centre.

In general, the family counselling centres in Norway are expanding, supported by the state through the Ministry of Social Affairs, and staffed by trained social workers. The state does not treat marriage counselling as a separate form of service, but as part of a general family counselling service, having a strong medical content. In 1953 the Norwegian Labour Party's National Women's Congress requested the Ministry of Social Affairs to help with the establishment of family counselling centres, and the increased support for this work dates from that time. Clients, it seems, go to whichever centre the think will best serve their needs, and the development of the Norwegian counselling service is still at an experimental stage. A major obstacle to further development is the shortage of skilled workers, and it is generally accepted that improved training facilities for counsellors are needed.

Sweden

In Sweden, as in the other Scandinavian countries, divorce is a comparatively simple process and, although 'divorce by consent' is not legally recognized, the established practice in fact amounts to this. If a couple wish to be divorced they will visit a lawyer and arrange the terms of a separation agreement. One year later the divorce is registered; this is a purely administrative matter, and it is not necessary to obtain a court order. It is possible to obtain a divorce rather more quickly by applying to a court, if either party has committed adultery or cruelty, has become an alcoholic or has been sent to prison.

Under the old common law of Sweden, if a man and his wife quarrelled, and if this became widely known, the local priest had a duty to admonish them in public. If they failed to mend their ways they could be fined by a local court. In 1860 a system of warning before the church council was substituted for the fine, and when divorce was later made legal it had to be preceded by warnings given first by the local priest and then by the church council. In 1915 the old procedures were abolished and a legal reconciliation system was set up. Some minor amendments to this system were made in 1946, 1951 and 1964, and Swedish law now provides a compulsory reconciliation procedure before any divorce on the grounds of separation can be registered.

Under this procedure, a reconciliator is appointed (there are about one thousand of them in Stockholm alone) whose duty it is to listen to both parties, to be impartial, and 'in a suitable way reconcile the parties'.[1] The mediator should have regard not only to the facts relating to the breakdown of the marriage, but also consider the conflicting emotions that have led to this situation.

This statutory provision was designed to prevent the unfortunate social consequences of divorce, and was introduced at the same time as divorce was made more easy. A conciliator may be a priest, a district judge, a man or woman appointed by the local authority for the purpose, or a person specially nominated by the husband or the wife. In fact, only a very small proportion of the conciliators make any serious attempt to reconcile the spouses. The normal procedure is for them to attend together before him for a few minutes. He takes particulars and asks whether there is any prospect of reconciliation; they reply that there is none, whereupon he gives them a certificate stating that he has seen them and can find no hope of reconciliation.

One of the reasons given for the somewhat spurious nature of this reconciliation procedure is that the mediators are only paid 15 Swedish *krone* (about 22s 6d) for each consultation and that this is not sufficient to persuade them to take the task at all seriously. Many of the appointed mediators are pastors, and some are lawyers, but the effect they appear to have on the Swedish divorce rate of 117 per 100,000 people seems to be negligible. Certainly the divorcing parties, and the legal profession in Sweden, do not regard the statutory reconciliation procedure as effective, or even as serious.

The almost total failure of this attempt at compulsory reconciliation is not, however, the only means of combating the increasing divorce problem in Sweden. In 1951, the Family Counselling Bureau of Stockholm was set up, and this bureau offers professional help in problems concerning marriage and the family, mainly by means of personal interviews. The Stockholm Bureau at present employs eleven professional social workers, most of whom have had psychological training. It operates from two centres, and is seeing over five hundred clients a year. The bureau is financed by the city authorities.

The government is now supporting several other family counselling centres in different parts of Sweden. The Ministry of

[1] *Swedish Law on Marriage.* Ch. 14, S. 3.

Health regard the work as still in an experimental stage, and it is only as recently as 1960 that government financial support has been provided. The Swedish Minister for Family Affairs then declared that 'the steadily increasing number of divorces and all the personal problems and differences they imply, not least for the children, underlines the importance of a type of family counselling that can be provided at a much earlier stage than the present compulsory mediation'. By 1966 nine centres had been set up in different parts of the country, and applications for grants in aid had been made by another six centres. The existing nine centres are staffed entirely by medically qualified men and women, and some of them are actually sited within existing hospital buildings.

The link between these centres and the Ministry of Health is tenuous, and their only direct responsibility is to submit annual reports to the ministry, giving particulars of the work done at the centre. The administration of the centres is in the hands of the communes, of which there are twenty-four in Sweden, and which compare roughly to the English county. The annual grants from the Ministry of Health are 6,000 *krone* for each doctor employed and 3,000 *krone* for each medically trained social worker; the communes have to bear the balance of the expense of maintaining the centres. At each centre there are normally two social workers, with a psychiatrist and a gynaecologist giving part-time help.

The service offered at these centres is on a pattern laid down by statute. No fee can be charged, and the clients can even be given money to help them make the journey to the counselling centre. All centres must provide at least one evening session weekly, presumably to ensure that working men have some opportunity to avail themselves of the service. It is government policy to expand this service as much as possible, but a major inhibiting factor is the lack of trained workers.

The Family Counselling Bureau in Stockholm, already referred to, has been working for over fifteen years and has acquired considerable status. It came into being before the government took action to set up the medical family counselling centres, and it is solely responsible to the Stockholm Child Welfare Board. The reason for its attachment to the Child Welfare Board is that the city council considered that the welfare of children was seriously affected by the breakdown of marriages, and decided to support the work of the bureau because its aim is to restore family relationships. It has already been mentioned that the bureau uses the services of eleven trained social workers, but it also pays four psychiatrists, a gynaecologist and a psycho-analytically trained psychologist as consultants. All these consultants work part-time at the bureau and are paid fees based on the amount of work done.

From the first contact with the bureau, the client has his own family counsellor allotted to him, and when possible the other partner is also invited to see this same counsellor. Following the preliminary interviews the clients may be referred for psychiatric help, or may embark on a series of regular interviews with the counsellor. Occasionally a second counsellor is allotted to work with the other partner, but normally one counsellor will see both husband and wife. Each case is discussed between all counsellors and consultants who are dealing with it, and some cases are brought up for consideration at the regular case discussions at which all the bureau's staff are present.

There has been an attempt to analyze the effect of the bureau's work. From this analysis it appears that in only 10 per cent of all cases seen did there appear to be no prospect of helping the clients. In another 16 per cent of cases it was possible to make useful referrals of clients to other organizations for specialized help not provided by the bureau, and a similar proportion of clients were given direct and practical help by the bureau on budgeting and housing problems. In a further 27 per cent of the cases the bureau was able to give support through fairly short-term counselling, which usually involved helping clients to adapt better to their environment, but did not involve long-term counselling. In the remaining and largest group, 31 per cent of the cases seen by the bureau, long-term counselling was given, sometimes involving psychiatric treatment. For many of these clients counselling extended over a period of a year or more.

It is notoriously difficult to assess the results of marriage counselling work, partly because no accepted criteria for 'success' or 'failure' have yet been established. For instance, the bureau by no means regards a case as a failure if, in spite of a divorce, the surrounding circumstances of the spouses have been eased and if life has been made less unpleasant for the children of the marriage. Bearing in mind these reservations, it is stated that from an analysis of a substantial number of cases that 7·8 per cent of the clients appeared to have resolved their problems entirely. Another 34·4 per cent had been helped to such an extent that the condition of their marriage seemed to have improved, and in 26 per cent of the cases there appeared to be no improvement. So far as the remaining cases were concerned (31·8 per cent) no evaluation was made, so it can be assumed that the condition of these marriages either deteriorated or that the bureau was unable to obtain information about them. Among the other facts emerging from the analysis, it appears that there was a greater prospect of improvement when both partners were willing to see a counsellor. This is perhaps not surprising, for when both partners are willing to attend they are frequently both interested in preserving the marriage.

Most clients make their first contact with the Stockholm Bureau by telephoning for an appointment, and the bureau's director normally reserves the time between 9 a.m. and 10 a.m. for this purpose. Some attempt is made at this stage to assess the nature of the client's problem, and she is then given an appointment with one of the caseworkers at the bureau. All the workers have received some form of social work training, and several have been involved in social work in other countries. Many of those who have done some prior social work training follow this, concurrently with their work at the bureau, with post-graduate courses in mental hygiene at Stockholm University. During their first year, all new workers at the bureau have the help and guidance of a supervisor.

At the present time all social workers at the bureau are women, probably because of the comparatively low salary paid to the staff. Social workers are normally recruited below the age of thirty, and each is paid about 250 Swedish *krone* per month. No volunteers are used, for in Sweden as a whole there is some suspicion of voluntary work. To the observer it seems as if voluntary work is associated essentially with the churches, and in this primarily secular society there is little value placed on work done by the volunteer. This has naturally led to a very severe shortage of workers, but the Swedes feel that it is essential that all family counsellors should not only be trained but also paid for the work they do, and that only in this way can standards of work be maintained. The original workers at the Stockholm bureau were recruited by a small committee, many of them being attracted to the work by the fact that it was a new kind of service.

The Stockholm bureau, in addition to its caseworkers, also employs a receptionist, a bookkeeper and other office staff, and the atmosphere at the centre is friendly and quite unlike that of a clinic or an office. All counselling is confidential, and clients can if they wish remain anonymous. A small number of those who come to the centre are allotted a number, and are not known by name.

Although the bureau has been working for over fifteen years, it feels it is still engaged in pioneering work. As an example of this, there is an increasing tendency for interviews at which husbands and wives attend together. Research projects are in hand in conjunction with the university, and there are plans to improve the tutorials given to the caseworkers. There is also a programme of marriage preparation, and for a small fee an engaged couple can attend courses consisting of at least five sessions. These usually start in September, and some continue until Christmas, depending on the wishes of the couples. The bureau also helps young couples who are expecting a baby but who are not sure whether it would be wise for them to marry. One reason why these couples come to the bureau is that it can sometimes help them to obtain the special permission to marry necessary under Swedish law for those under the normal legal minimum age for marriage.

Some of the counsellors working at the bureau are permitted to act as conciliators under the provisions of Swedish reconciliation law, but the bureau is not at all anxious to attract large numbers of clients who come under the compulsory reconciliation procedure, as it does not feel that this is the best atmosphere in which counselling work can be done.

Finland

In common with Norway and Sweden, Finland has enacted a law making provision for marital reconciliation, but this law applies only to one of the three main means of obtaining a divorce. In the first place, some divorces are granted on the grounds that a matrimonial offence, such as adultery, cruelty or alcoholism, has taken place, in which case no attempt at reconciliation need be shown before a divorce is granted to the petitioner. Secondly, it is possible to obtain a divorce without difficulty when the husband and wife have been separated from one another for more than two years. The third basis for divorce is a period of separation for at least one year, following a court decree of judicial separation, and it is this decree that must by law be preceded by some attempt at reconciliation.

Under this law, the husband and wife must see an official conciliator together, and must later visit him individually. These interviews must take place within a period of one month, and the conciliator may then issue a certificate that he has seen the couple and has found that there appears to be no prospect of a reconciliation. The conciliator's duty is to make clear to the couple the social, financial and other consequences that will flow from a divorce, if this is the course they wish to take.

All leading pastors of the Established Church of Finland, the Lutheran Church, are automatically appointed as official conciliators, and in 1965 there were 346 of these pastors throughout Finland. About 92 per cent of the population of Finland is regarded as belonging to the Lutheran Church. However, only a very small proportion of the people are active members of it, and in many cases the task of the pastor/conciliator is a mere formality.

Social workers responsible to the Department of Social Welfare make up another 225 official conciliators, and a recent amendment of the law has resulted in a further 350 counsellors attached to the various family counselling centres being added to the number. There are now over 900 official conciliators in Finland, a country where about 3,500 divorces take place each year. The great majority of the pastor/conciliators work in the Helsinki area, but the other official conciliators are spread more evenly over the rest of the country.

The social workers who act as conciliators also do other social work, and receive a salary. They are trained for their work, and visit homes in their area as part of their general responsibility for family care. They are normally responsible to the local director of social services, who is in turn responsible to the county authority. Ultimately, the Ministry of Social Affairs has final responsibility for the work, which includes a certain amount of marriage counselling. It is often found, as in other countries, that family problems involving the children stem from a breakdown in the relationship between husband and wife.

A large organization undertaking a considerable amount of family work in Finland is the Population and Family Welfare League (*Vaestoliitto*). This is an independent agency deriving almost the whole of its income from a large state lottery. The income of the lottery comes from machines placed in all restaurants and cafes throughout Finland, and large sums of money are paid from the profits of this lottery to several organizations. The Population and Family Welfare League, originally supported mainly by a government grant, now relies almost entirely on the lottery income to carry on its work. The government is represented on the lottery board, and has some influence on the way in which its grants are made. A similar scheme is operated in New Zealand (see Chapter 6).

Almost two-thirds of the work of the league involves giving family planning advice, and rather less than a quarter of its workers' time is spent with married people who are experiencing emotional and sexual difficulties in their marriages. All workers at the league are medically qualified, either as psychiatrists, psychologists, gynaecologists or nurses, and they wear white overalls while doing their work, even if this is only a counselling interview and not a medical examination. There are at present four clinics at which the league's work is carried on, and in the country as a whole about 500 clients are helped each year with marriage problems of an emotional and sexual nature.

The league's clinics are used as the main means of obtaining a legal abortion in Finland, and quite frequently it is found that the women who come seeking an abortion also have marriage problems. Because the clinics operate over a very wide area of family service it is unusual for them to have to refer their patients, as they term them, to other social service agencies. Every aspect of the league's work is increasing, but each year brings a greater increase in the amount of family planning than in other work. Some 93 per cent of the population of the country speak Finnish, and the remainder (mostly in the south-west) speak Swedish, so there is another but much smaller Population and Welfare League giving a similar service to this minority group.

The other large organization undertaking marriage counselling work in Finland is the Lutheran Church, not through its pastors, but through nine family counselling centres which it has set up in different parts of the country. These centres are controlled by the Church Board of Family Affairs, which is financed from the central funds of the Lutheran Church. The Church's income, and thus the income of the nine counselling centres, is derived from a national Church tax, roughly equivalent to the former system of tithes in England. The Lutheran Church being the Established State Church, a tax of one per cent on income is collected from all Church members. The tax is collected at the same time as the income tax paid to the state, and is sufficient to support most of the Church's work in Finland, including the operation of the family counselling centres. The Church Board of Family Affairs is planning to establish another three counselling centres as soon as possible. The board is not connected with the Ministry of Social Affairs or with any other branch of the government.

The first development of counselling work began in 1944 in the town of Tampere, where the Reverend Matti Joensuu succeeded in obtaining funds to set up a small centre where he was able to offer a family counselling service with the help of a psychiatrist and a lawyer. In 1945 a similar centre was founded in Helsinki; some thirty clergymen acted as counsellors, on a part-time basis and without payment. The only salaried member at the Helsinki centre at that time was a secretary, who arranged appointments and acted as receptionist. Up until this time, no form of training existed for marriage counselling as such, but this was then instituted in the Helsinki centre. There were many initial difficulties, for several members of the clergy had found the work too hard and lost confidence in their ability to help clients. In 1949, Mr Joensuu was appointed full-time director of the Helsinki centre and did most of the counselling work himself, with the assistance of professional volunteers. Two years later he visited England, and there studied the work which was being developed by the National Marriage Guidance Council. He found that much of the experience then gained in England was similar to his own, and on his return to Finland he introduced a method of using selected and trained volunteers on the British pattern.

The first counsellors in Helsinki, twelve in all, worked for some years, but the centre became gradually convinced that it was taking too long for them to become sufficiently skilled, and ultimately decided to use only full-time workers. The change from part-time volunteers to full-time paid workers was made gradually, and most counsellors now work full-time. In 1953, almost ten years after the first centre had been opened, the Lutheran Church decided to accept that family counselling and family life education were a task of the Church, and Mr Joensuu was appointed its secretary for family affairs.

The counselling work of the Church is done on entirely modern lines, and indeed has aroused a certain amount of opposition among the more conservative elements in the Lutheran Church. However, one of the booklets describing the work of the centres states 'it is also our task in the centres to preach the Gospel of the boundless resources of God and of the redemption between God and man and among men'. This is interpreted by those running the Helsinki centre, which employs eleven counsellors, as meaning that the counselling work is an expression of the religious beliefs of the workers. They state that no attempt is made to preach the Gospel to clients, but clients of course know that the centres are linked with the Church. In one, but only in one, of the counselling rooms of the Helsinki centre there is a statuette of Christ. Several of the counsellors employed there are ordained ministers of the Lutheran Church.

The Board selects and trains all its counsellors. As the work is reasonably well paid there are often several applications for each post that falls vacant, and all candidates are interviewed by a psychiatrist, a psychologist and an experienced counsellor. They also take a written intelligence test and a personality test, and must have already had some form of professional training, e.g. in medicine, law or psychology. After appointment they undergo a further period of training lasting a year. The first part of this training is theoretical and the remainder practical, the new counsellor working with his clients under the supervision of a tutor.

Each counselling centre, in addition to the counsellors' services, can call on the professional help of a psychiatrist and a lawyer. Each of the smaller centres costs the Church Board about forty thousand Finnish *marks* a year, and is run by a local board of directors. The centres state that they have a friendly relationship with the other social services, and frequently refer clients to mental hospitals, when this is appropriate. They also work closely with alcoholic clinics, who themselves often have to cope with marriage and other family problems. Each centre of reasonable size has regular case discussions, attended by the counsellors and a psychiatrist. There are now sixteen people working full-time in the nine centres, ten of whom are members of the clergy. In addition, there are ten workers who have been fully trained and who work on average three days a week.

Most clients come to the centres after telephoning for an appointment. Roughly half the cases are seen on a short-term basis (one or two interviews) but the remaining cases are helped over a longer term. It has been found that about 70 per cent of the clients are formal, but not active, members of the Lutheran church, and it seems that those people who do not want to have any connection with the Church tend to go elsewhere if they need help with marriage difficulties. Nevertheless, the work of all the centres is expanding considerably. In 1956, 1,148 clients were given a total of 1,950 interviews, a rather low average of 1·7 interviews per client. The comparative figures for 1966 were 3,594 clients and 11,847 interviews, an average of 3·3 interviews per client, which compares closely with similar figures for counselling work in Britain and in Australia. No client is expected to pay any fee for the help he receives. About two-thirds of the clients are women, and most clients are aged between twenty-five and forty-five when first seen by a counsellor. Of the women clients, about two-thirds are earning a salary, and in fact the great majority of the clients are from the higher social categories. The actual figures given by the centres are as follows:

Social Category I	15·5%
Social Category II	24·0%
Social Category III	48·0%
Remainder, being unskilled workers and students	12·5%

The Church Family Board is at present pursuing research into the effectiveness of the marriage counselling work, and has recently started on a programme of education for family life. This new work is mostly being done by volunteers, and is still at an early stage of development. The board finds that it is also being called upon to help in training young Lutheran pastors in social work, and arranges special training courses for other Church members.

The impression gained is that family and marriage counselling work in Finland is fairly highly developed, especially so when one realizes that the country has only recently emerged from the extremely difficult conditions created by the 1939-45 war, during which the Finns were at war at different times with Russia, with Great Britain and with Germany. The population of the country is only a little over four million, but marriage counselling work has developed further than similar work in the other Scandinavian countries.

Denmark

In Denmark, the law relating to divorce is similar to that in the other Scandinavian countries and in Finland. An immediate divorce can be obtained in cases of adultery or severe cruelty committed by one spouse; after a period of two and a half years' separation either party can obtain a divorce, and this period is reduced to one and a half years if the separation took place by agreement and was duly recognized by the state. Some changes in the Danish divorce law are at present being considered which would have the effect of abolishing adultery as a ground for divorce.

To obtain an official separation recognized by the state the couple have to visit a local government official, or if they live in the Copenhagen area will usually go to the Copenhagen Praesidium, a branch of the city council. The law provides that if the couple are members of the State Church they must visit their local pastor, who will ask them if there is any chance of reconciliation, and may possibly try to persuade them not to go ahead with the divorce. It is in fact possible for both parties to be ordered to see the pastor, even if one or both of them is reluctant, but it is clear that this procedure rarely, if ever, results in a reconciliation.

The local government officer who sees the couple seeking an official separation has a duty to inform them of the legal and other consequences of a divorce, and records the agreed terms of the separation. The agreement will cover such matters as the custody of children, the division of property, and the financial provision that the husband is to make for his wife. Normally these matters can be agreed, at any rate after discussions with the officer, but if there is no agreement the parties can apply to a court to settle the matter.

It seems quite clear that, in spite of the legal provisions relating to reconciliation by the pastors, this procedure has almost no effect. In the first place, the great majority of the couples visiting the pastor are not regular church-goers, and secondly the element of compulsion is of no help in reconciling husband and wife. It may well be that this attempt at reconciliation comes too late in the day, and that action that might have helped the marriage would have best been applied at a much earlier stage.

There is a national organization in Denmark known as the Mothers' Aid which gives practical help to married people with difficulties, but this is mainly confined to instruction in personal hygiene, housekeeping methods and other financial matters. There is also an organization known as the Christian Association for Child Care, existing mainly to help young people with family problems, in particular those parents who have children needing special care. The association naturally meets several families where the marriage relationship is breaking down, and some attempt is made to help in such cases. However, the main work of this association is with children, and not with parents.

It is therefore left mainly to the family centres and to the new Family Guidance Council to provide what skilled marriage counselling facilities there are in Denmark. At present their work is not very well known, and in fact some government departments do not seem to be aware of their existence, or at any rate of the fact that they are offering a marriage counselling service. The family centres have been in existence for upwards of five years, and in Copenhagen there are separate centres for each division of the city. At one centre in the poorest part of Copenhagen there are six social workers, two of whom work full-time, and all of whom are paid. A psychologist attends for half a day each week, and all the social workers have one tutorial session with him weekly, as well as the usual case discussions with one another. A psychiatrist attends very occasionally, as a consultant. The psychologist is responsible for the administration of the centre, which is controlled by a board consisting of a representative of the city council, two psychologists, a doctor in general practice, a pastor, a schoolteacher and a child care officer.

Most clients coming to this centre are women, and many of them have to go out to work because their husbands are alcoholics. Most of the work is done in the clients' homes, and not at the family centre. No fees are charged, and there is usually a waiting list. The centre is financed by the city of Copenhagen, and may well become merged before long with the Family Guidance Council. The social workers have all had some form of training, but this has been variable in extent, which makes continuous in-service training all the more important. The centre co-operates with other social services and with the professions, but the tendency in Copenhagen is for all services dealing with the family to become centralized, and it appears likely that the Family Guidance Council will ultimately take over the others.

The Family Guidance Council of Copenhagen, founded as recently as 1965, is intended to serve as a pattern for the establishment of similar centres in other parts of Denmark, and there is already an effective Council operating in Aarhus, in Jutland, linked to an existing social work training college. The new Council is setting high standards for its workers, each of whom is paid 2,200 kroner a month (about £120). Candidates for the work, aged between thirty and fifty, are expected to have a background of experience in some kind of social work, and to attend a form of selection conference. In the first year 320 people applied for jobs and twenty-five were selected; during training, a few of the latter have been asked to withdraw from the work. The social workers can refer for help to a psychiatrist, a psychologist or a lawyer, all of whom are attached to the Copenhagen centre and are paid for their services.

The Council has been in some difficulty in its first year because of the relationship between its workers and the representatives of political parties in the capital. From the year 1933 it became the practice in Denmark for political parties to send people to visit families whose members had been convicted of criminal offences. Many of these people attracted to this work were ladies of fairly advanced years, often well off, and almost entirely without training for social work. The new Council is required to work with these voluntary political workers, and does not always find the relationship an easy one. In fact, it seems that it is because this work has been in the hands of unselected and untrained voluntary workers so long that it has not developed as fully in Denmark as it has in the other Scandinavian countries.

It appears that the Family Guidance Council had some initial difficulties, and found it hard to attract clients in the early months, but by the end of the first year it was dealing with over 1,000 cases, each social worker having a case-load of not more than twenty-five cases. The main work of the Council is not with married couples, but with the mothers of young children who are living alone, either because they are not married or because they have been deserted or are divorced. Out of 600 cases recently handled by the Council, 525 involved mothers living alone with their children. The remaining seventy-five cases (12·5 per cent of the total) were married couples in need of help, and these couples were seen by one of the Council's social workers. Mothers and their children are normally seen in their homes, but marriage counselling is done at the Copenhagen centre.

The majority of the married people are seen by appointment, and many of them have been encouraged to come to the centre by the Copenhagen Praesidium, or by other social work agencies in Copenhagen. There are also an increasing number of referrals from doctors and lawyers, and also from the more liberal-minded clergy, as the work of the Council is becoming better known. The Council plans to expand its marriage counselling service not only in Copenhagen but also in centres in other parts of Denmark. At present the work is necessarily at an early stage of development, but the considerable use of the Council's services in the first year indicates the need that exists.

The Council is financed wholly by the Copenhagen city council, which receives a grant from the state to enable this to be done. There is in fact no shortage of funds, because all money necessary for the employment of social workers, and for the administration of the Council, is automatically provided on request. This must be one of the very few organizations in any part of the world that is so fortunate in this respect, and it may be that the reason is not so much the value placed on a marriage counselling service as on the importance of helping unmarried or deserted mothers. The establishment of this new Council, and the possibility of similar centres being opened in other parts of the country, is due to a change of policy at the Danish Ministry of Social Affairs, which is now placing more emphasis than formerly on support for the family, and especially for the children.

Chapter 8

UNITED STATES OF AMERICA — GENERAL

Counselling Services and Family Courts
There are many marriage counselling services provided in the United States. These range from the professional work of individual practitioners, through that of family service agencies, church and other community organizations, to the services provided by the courts and other authorities of the various States. The short survey that follows is by no means comprehensive, but it describes in outline the main different types of marriage counselling services that exist. For convenience, the operation of the fast-growing conciliation courts is described in the next chapter.

The first organized marriage counselling services in the United States began in the year 1928, under the guidance of Dr Emily Mudd in Philadelphia and Dr Paul Popenoe in Los Angeles. It was in Philadelphia that the phrase 'marriage counseling' seems first to have been coined.

American Association of Marriage Counselors
This Association was founded in 1942, and its executive directors between 1960 and 1967 were Professor and Mrs David Mace. Professor Mace was previously secretary of the National Marriage Guidance Council in Great Britain. The Association is the only nationally recognized professional organization operating in this field; it has long taken an uncompromising stand for high qualifications on the part of all its members, who can set up as private practitioners and can charge whatever fees they wish for the counselling services they offer. In a country where there are many less competent and less scrupulous people purporting to offer marriage counselling, membership of the Association is highly prized.

The purpose of the Association is to foster the exchange of

relevant information and to provide and maintain standards in the new professional field of marriage counselling. In order to qualify for membership of the Association, candidates must first be fully accredited members of what is termed a 'helping profession', that is, medicine, social work, the church or psychology. They must also have had additional training in the practice of personal counselling or in psychotherapy, and have been supervised for at least one year in marriage counselling as such. Finally, members must have had at least two years' experience, on at least a half-time basis, as practising marriage counsellors. This enables them to qualify as associate members, and they need five years' experience as practising counsellors to entitle them to apply for full membership. The Association has an admissions committee, which may ask candidates for written case material, personal interviews and oral examinations. It also operates a nationwide mail referral service; enquirers are referred only to members of the Association, or to agencies of the highest repute.

In the year 1955 an investigation of the professions of Association members showed that the medical profession represented one third of the membership. In addition, 18 per cent of members were ministers of religion, 16 per cent social workers, 13 per cent psychologists, 11 per cent sociologists and 11 per cent were members of the teaching profession. By 1966 there had been a considerable change in professional allegiance, psychologists representing 26 per cent of the membership and social workers 25 per cent. At the present time there are rather less than 2,000 members of the Association. In 1967, Professor Mace and his wife resigned as part-time executive directors, and their place was taken by a full-time salaried director, Edward J. Rydman, Ph.D.

The Association has a code of professional ethics, and any complaints against members are investigated by a committee. Several centres in the United States are offering training facilities to the standards set by the Association, and two of these centres receive grants from the Federal Government through the National Institute for Mental Health. Trainees at these centres are required to work with clients during their training courses, as members of a team, under close supervision by tutors. Once trained, counsellors may decide to work in private practice, become attached to one of the conciliation courts, to a family service agency or other organization, or to a group of churches. Some have been taken into partnership by medical practitioners.

There are therefore very few people in the United States undertaking marriage counselling without payment, and many of those who do so are looked upon with suspicion. The average American expects to pay for all services that he receives, and marriage counselling is no exception. Indeed, many clients would not feel that the counsellor was likely to possess much skill if he did not charge a fee, or was not paid by an agency for his services.

In spite of an increasing number of training courses and a growing number of marriage counsellors, there is still a very real shortage. This is shown in the reports from the various family service agencies and the conciliation courts, who almost all speak of the need to obtain more trained staff. One of the problems created by this shortage of counsellors has been that a large number of unqualified and unskilled people have moved into a field where profits are large and where there is no law preventing them from describing themselves as marriage counsellors. Some of these people advertise their services in the press and, to quote Professor Mace, 'conceal their incompetence by the purchase of spurious degrees'. One of the results of this malpractice has been a growing pressure for protective legislation, and some States have already passed laws for the certification of marriage counsellors operating within their boundaries. California was the first State to do this, and more recently the State of Michigan enacted similar legislation. The statutes normally provide that communications between counsellor and client are privileged from disclosure in a court of law, unless the counsellor is defending himself against a charge of malpractice, or is reporting to the court following a referral it has made to him.

Private Practice

Many members of the American Association of Marriage Counselors are in private practice as counsellors. A large number of those counsellors already working in family service agencies or other institutions would like to establish themselves in private practice, often because the caseloads they have to carry are higher than they would wish. Moreover, in the United States the private practitioner often has higher status than the counsellor working for an agency. There are, however, many difficulties facing the would-be practitioner; he cannot be assured of a regular income if he moves into private practice, and very often he may feel more confidence in his ability to operate as a counsellor than as a man in business on his own account.

Some counsellors try to make the best of both worlds, by developing a private practice at the same time as working for an agency. Their first step will usually be to associate with colleagues in the same or related professions. This is more likely to be successful than a sudden move into private practice, which will not produce enough immediate referrals. It is through personal referrals of one kind or another that many professional people live, and this is particularly so for the private practitioner in marriage counselling.

For the private practitioner to operate successfully he will have to acquire attractive premises, pay rent and meet other expenses, employ a secretary to make appointments and to do other office work. Out of his income he must make arrangements for his own pension, unlike the counsellor who has been employed by an agency operating a pension scheme. There are other restrictions: when he takes a holiday his income temporarily ceases; he will find that he has to work a good deal in the evenings, because this is the time when many of his male clients can come to see him. He will become conscious of being over-dependent for his income on the fees paid by a comparatively small number of clients who come to see him regularly week by week, which may tempt him to extend the counselling longer than is really necessary.

The most natural protection against these hazards is for the practitioner to form an association with colleagues, sometimes other marriage counsellors, but frequently members of other professions. This happens most frequently when the counsellor already has a medical or other qualification, in addition to his experience and training as a marriage counsellor. One such association is the Counseling and Psychotherapy Center at Fair Lawn, New Jersey, the executive director of which is Thomas C. McGinnis, Ed. D. Dr McGinnis is attached to New York University as instructor in marriage and the family, and is a member of the American Psychological Association, and currently treasurer of the American Association of Marriage Counselors. The New Jersey centre also makes use of the services of a psychiatric consultant.

Family Service Agencies
There are well over three hundred family service agencies in the United States of America and Canada, all of them members of the Family Service Association of America. All these agencies provide marriage counselling services, as well as other help to the community. The agencies are situated in the main population areas, on the Eastern seaboard of the United States, in the area south of the Great Lakes and in California, and they all use professionally trained workers. The focus is on the family as a unit, and on the individual members of the family.

The Family Service Association of America, with its headquarters in New York, exists to set standards for the operation of these family service agencies, and is also working for the improvement of social conditions for all families. It undertakes research work, helps its member agencies with administrative problems, co-operates with other national organizations and publishes material relevant to its work. Member agencies can be either governmental or voluntary. If governmental, to become members of the Association they must either have a board or an advisory committee representing the interests of the local community.

In fact, the great majority of the member agencies of the Association are voluntary organizations, deriving the greater part of their income from private sources, and conforming to the standards laid down by the Association. Member agencies must have a board of directors of reasonable size, representative of the community, and also the resources to fulfil their main purposes. They also assume responsibility for fund-raising, and must be adequately housed and staffed. The staff must include at least one trained caseworker, an executive director and a secretary. Many agencies, of course, have far more staff than this. Agencies are expected by the Family Service Association to participate in its general affairs, to work towards the improvement of social conditions which have a negative effect on family life, and to evolve a community education programme. Before achieving full membership status they have to have provided an adequate service for at least a year, and are required to send to the Association an evaluation of this work. This is normally done by means of the agency's annual report. There is provision for agencies who are hoping to achieve membership to become pre-membership affiliates.

The Association argues the need for its work on the fact that the marriages of over 750,000 people a year in the United States end in divorce, and also on the large number of delinquent children and illegitimate births. In the early days of the Association, social work was still being done by voluntary unpaid workers, but voluntary effort is now confined to the management boards of the agencies. No doubt as a result of the efforts of these volunteers, over two-thirds of the income of family service agencies comes from charitable foundations of one kind or another. Fees from clients account for about 7 per cent of income, and reimbursements from public funds slightly less than this.

The local agencies often serve a particular part of the community. As an example, there is the Jewish Family Service of Los Angeles. It employs over twenty professional caseworkers, has the services of three psychiatrists as part-time consultants, and provides field work and supervision for students from the nearby school of social work. This Service is financially supported by a Jewish charity in Los Angeles, United Way Inc., and also by the United Jewish Welfare Fund. Fees are charged to those who are able to pay, and the amount of these varies according to the income of the family being helped.

Another example is the Family Service Association of San Diego, California, which operates in a very similar way to the Jewish family service, but without religious affiliation. It provides, in addition to marriage counselling, help for couples who are anxious about their children. Counselling is also offered to those who have already divorced or separated. The San Diego Association charges fees, which range from $1 for the first two interviews in the case of someone earning not more than $250 a month, to $15 for someone earning over $700 a month. If regular counselling follows the original consultation, fees are graded according to income and size of family. The San Diego agency also provides group counselling, and makes a charge for this as well, payments being normally made before the sessions start. The agency produces a leaflet describing its work, entitled *Marriage and Family Counseling.*

Some agencies operating in rural areas are using mobile offices. In Oakland County, Michigan, a large vehicle, 27 feet long, is used. It has been especially designed for counselling work, and is divided into two parts, one for use as an interviewing room and the other as a waiting room. The caseworker drives the vehicle, which was bought for the agency by a local charitable foundation for $9,000. It costs $100 a month to run, the same cost as the rent of an office.

The Family Service Association of America has issued its own guide for communities who wish to start a new agency. This sets out the essential elements in the provision of a service, as already described, and states that the impetus for establishing an agency must come from a group of citizens who recognize the need for it. The Association has field consultants who visit the areas where agencies are being set up. The consultant's task is to investigate other resources in the community to see whether an agency is really needed and, if there seems to be a case for establishing one, to encourage the formation of a steering committee. This committee is expected to recruit members and to produce documentary evidence of the need, which is usually done by circularizing local professional people with a questionnaire. A report is then issued with the intention of gaining publicity through the press, television and radio.

Having done its work and set up the agency, the steering committee disbands itself, and its place is taken by a board of directors, several of whom are likely to be members of the original committee. There are normally a minimum of twenty-one members of the board of directors, and the Association encourages agencies to have many more than that number of individual members. The first meeting of members elects the board, who have then to plan a programme of work, produce a budget and recruit staff. Normally they will first engage an executive director, whose job will then be to find suitable premises and the remaining staff. The Association reminds its members of the many expenses that will be involved in starting the agency, including payments to professional consultants and affiliation fees due to the National Association, as well as ordinary running costs and salaries. The premises used by agencies are often in commercial or municipal buildings, but sometimes in converted private houses.

The work programme of each individual agency depends on the area it is to serve and the kind of people who live there. Arrangements for making appointments are worked out, and a special committee is set up to cover public relations work. It is found that about 10 per cent of all clients are self-referred, but that the majority are sent to the agency by friends or neighbours, by other social organizations or by schools, churches and the courts. The higher the social class of the applicant, the more likely he is to come direct to the agency. Over half the applicants for the first interview are married women; in just under a quarter of cases the husband and wife come together, and husbands who come alone to the agencies represent only 17 per cent of first interviews. Nearly one half of all applications to the agencies are for marriage counselling; the remainder are for help with other family problems.

The Association is presently working on a project which is intended to assess the underlying processes involved in the solution or alleviation of marriage difficulties, and this project is supported by a grant from the National Institute of Mental Health. An adjunct to this project is a scheme to improve the in-service training, and therefore the skills, of practising counsellors. In addition, management training courses are run by the Association, each normally lasting a week. The courses are attended by the executive directors of family service agencies, and are run in association with the Columbia University Graduate School of Business.

The affiliation fees paid by the member agencies account for about half the income of the National Association. A quarter of its income comes from the sale of various publications, and most of the remainder is made up by special grants from other bodies. The Association grows steadily, fifty nine new member agencies having joined in the period from January 1959 to June 1965.

Family Courts

We now turn to the marriage counselling service operated by family courts in various States. These courts are financed by the particular State, and are in effect operating a form of social service under the direction of the judges who are themselves elected, and responsible to the county authorities. Legislation enabling these family courts to be set up has been enacted in several States.

Toledo, Ohio. The family court of Lucas County, at Toledo, Ohio, has been built up over a period of many years. It comprises a probation department which deals with young offenders, a remand home for the young, and a marriage counselling department. The court was first opened in 1938, and in 1948 the services it was then operating were re-housed. The marriage counselling service was among the first to operate in the United States. In 1951 the State Legislature of Ohio passed a statute under which a court investigation into the 'character, family relations, past conduct, earning ability and financial worth of the parties to the action' was made obligatory in all divorce cases where a child of under fourteen years was involved. In 1955 a judge was appointed to take charge of the court work arising from this provision, and in 1964 a second judge had to be appointed to cope with the growing amount of work. In the State of Ohio there are at least seventeen such family courts.

The marriage counselling department at Toledo was originally known as the domestic relations department, and the judges attached to the family court dealt with both juvenile and matrimonial cases. Out of a total of 1,699 cases coming before the family court for investigation in one recent year, 1,425 arose under the provisions of the state law mentioned above; others included investigations undertaken on behalf of other state courts. There were also some post-divorce investigations, and a small amount of voluntary counselling work. In the majority of the cases referred to the department, namely those where a child under fourteen is involved, the petitioner is obliged by law to attend and see one of the counsellors attached to the court. His or her partner is at the same time offered a counselling interview. Counsellors make their own appointments with clients. Each counsellor has his own office, and no fees are payable by clients, as the service is operated by a public department.

Most counsellors at the Toledo court are members of the American Association of Marriage Counselors. One counsellor, who when engaged by the court had no experience of marriage

counselling, was interviewed by her prospective casework supervisor, by the judge and also by the court psychiatrist before
being offered a post. She then began work in conjunction with
in-service training lasting two months. At first she was handling
clients only under supervision, but by the end of two years was
permitted to carry a full caseload. At any time she was able to
consult other colleagues. The counsellor is British and, when she
returned to England, she took up work as a voluntary counsellor
with a Marriage Guidance Council in the north of the country.

The counsellors at Toledo are all officers of the court, and
make reports of all mandatory court investigations to the judge.
He has these reports in front of him at the time of hearing of the
divorce petition, but they tend to be of a general nature and do
not in normal circumstances deal with the details of the case.
The counsellor's report consists of an assessment of the marriage
in terms of its potential success or failure, and he is not expected
to produce a report using legal phraseology. His report will contain recommendations regarding the support of the wife and
children, and these recommendations are usually accepted by the
court. The position of the counsellor is somewhat analogous to
that of the probation officer in a British court. The counsellors
see it as part of their duty, where a divorce is inevitable, to
enable the parties to accept a reasonable settlement in a friendly
atmosphere. This is normally done during discussion between
the counsellors and the lawyers acting for the parties.

Many clients maintain contact with their counsellors over a
long period. Of 2,047 cases recently studied in a period of twelve
months, 481 were still in contact with counsellors over two
years after their application first came before the court, and
1,137 were in contact for more than six months. Only 546 cases
broke off all contact within the first thirty days. The report of
the court indicates that about 25 per cent of the families coming
before it appear to reach some kind of reconciliation. In other
cases, financial plans can be agreed, also arrangements for
custody of and access to children. In only 205 cases, 10 per cent
of those closed during the year, was no change in circumstances
or attitude noted. Admittedly these assessments are made by the
counsellors themselves, and they are unlikely to take a pessi-
mistic view of their own work, but there seems to be little doubt
that a service of real value to the community is being provided

in Toledo, not only where reconciliations are effected, but also where help is given to the parties to reach an amicable settlement in a reasonably calm atmosphere. In the United States as a whole, approximately 30 per cent of divorce petitions are later abandoned, but in Toledo the figure is 40 per cent and it seems at least possible that this increase is due in some measure to the work of the court.

About two-fifths of the clients who have been obliged to see the counsellors return voluntarily, and the court believes that only a shortage of counsellors prevents this proportion from being higher. Some petitioners dislike having to attend the counsellor, and one litigant was heard to say that the judge had 'sentenced him to counselling'. In spite of this kind of extreme opposition, the average number of interviews per client is five. The number of contacts for each case averages nine, but this includes consultations with the parties' lawyers. After psychotherapeutic counselling, which averages eight to ten interviews for each client, referrals are normally made to a social agency unattached to the court.

The family court does not provide the only marriage counselling service in Toledo; there are other social agencies in the town, such as the Lutheran Welfare Service, the Child and Family Service, the Toledo Catholic Charities and others who employ professional workers. These workers and the family court maintain regular contact with one another. On the whole, the professions in Toledo co-operate with the family court. A few lawyers are hostile, but this is to be expected in any community. The marriage counselling services are seen, by a minority of lawyers, as a threat to the livelihood they make through divorce work.

One unusual procedure in the Toledo service is the contact maintained with the client's legal adviser. This results from the status of the family court and of its counsellors, who provide a form of social service to the community at large, and at its expense. In other systems operating in the United States it is unusual for there to be any formal contact with the parties' lawyers, although many referrals from lawyers are made. One useful result of the formal contact in Toledo is the satisfactory settlement of some outstanding practical issues linked with the divorce proceedings, which saves their having to be adjudicated by the court. Ralph Bridgman, for several years chief marriage counsellor at Toledo, has explained the functions of the family court as 'the law and social welfare working together at the courts to protect and foster family life'.

Cook County, Illinois. In the State of Illinois, at the Circuit Court of Cook County, which includes Chicago, different attempts have been made to promote reconciliation over recent years. First, provision was made for a 'cooling-off' period, which ensured that time elapsed between the commencement of divorce proceedings and the date of their trial. Another amendment of the law permitted litigants to return to live together during attempts at reconciliation without the grounds for divorce being barred on the grounds of condonation. In 1964, a Conciliation Service was set up to operate in conjunction with the work of the divorce court.

Counselling is voluntary, no litigant being obliged to see a counsellor. All counsellors are professionally qualified and normally see the parties twice, sometimes for as long as two and a half hours on each occasion. If reconciliation has not been effected by then, but there appears still to be some hope of it, the parties are referred to one of the counselling agencies in Illinois; there are over twenty of these. Referral is also made from time to time to qualified marriage counsellors in private practice on their own account, and to psychologists and psychiatrists.

It is normal for both parties, and their lawyers, to sign a statement before counselling starts confirming that nothing said during the counselling sessions will later be made available for proceedings in the court. The lawyers are not excluded by law from the counselling sessions, but in practice they do not attend, as the intention of the counselling service is to reduce the adversary atmosphere. This is explained to clients in a pamphlet entitled, *Are you eligible for reconciliation counseling?*, which is handed to all divorce petitioners. The pamphlet states: 'The parties must be ready to save the marriage. They must have the proper attitude.' Clearly there is no inducement to use the services other than the prospect of reconciliation.

The counselling service is financed by the board of commissioners for Cook County, to whom the circuit court is also responsible. The board is an elected body, empowered to raise money by taxation. All counsellors are employed by the board, which also bears the administrative costs of the service. Administration includes reception of clients, making appointments, giving general information, keeping records and preparing statistics, and maintaining contact with other organizations. The staff of the service also look after the children of clients who bring them to the centre when visiting the counsellors. A trained legal secretary, who has had additional training in psychology, is in charge of the administration of the service. The secretary's additional duties include contact with the newspapers, radio and television, writing articles about the work of the service, assessing the statistical material and planning for the future.

In the first year of its work, the service helped 572 families. Of these, 243 were regarded as having been reconciled; 132 families failed to reconcile, and the remaining 197 were still being helped at the end of the year under review. Over 1,500 children were involved in these 572 cases. The number of reconciliations is recorded as having risen steadily during the year, but it is difficult to make an accurate assessment of the effectiveness of the service at this early stage of development.

Milwaukee, Wisconsin. The family court of Milwaukee, Wisconsin, was established in 1935, and has two judges working full-time handling domestic cases. A conciliation department is one of the social services operated by the court, and it is using eleven trained counsellors. Their functions are, so far as is possible, to reconcile estranged couples and harmonize disturbed family relations, and to investigate matters relating to the custody of children. A unique feature of the law of the State of Wisconsin is that an effort to reconcile the parties has to be made in every case, and this accounts for the large staff employed by the conciliation department. The State law also provides for a sixty-day 'cooling off' period to elapse between the date of filing the divorce petition and the date of hearing.

During the first twenty-five years of the life of the Milwaukee court, referrals for reconciliation were made selectively; the conciliation department only saw the parties if the court felt that prospects for reconciliation were good, or if they asked for counselling. In 1960 the law was changed, and the Wisconsin family code took effect. Now, every divorce case is referred to the department. Both husband and wife are directed to come for an interview, and if the petitioner does not attend the department the case will not come on for trial. Interviews are confidential, and only the fact that they have taken place is reported to the court. The court, having operated this new compulsory system for several years, is firmly of the opinion that it is best to require all divorce litigants to discuss the situation with a counsellor before the case comes up for trial.

In 1964, for every 100 divorce cases filed, 48 were dismissed because the petitioner did not proceed or because the parties agreed not to divorce. As has been mentioned, 30 per cent of all divorce petitions in the United States do not in fact result in divorce, but the Milwaukee figure is well above the national average. Before 1960 the percentage of cases not proceeding to trial was 39. There has thus been a rise of 9 per cent of such cases following the adoption of the Wisconsin family code. Not all dismissals represent reconciliations, and not all reconciliations last, but the fact remains that the percentage of cases pressed to a conclusion has dropped substantially.

The court admits that in many cases the enforced attendance at court will not help to mend the marriage or improve relationships between husband and wife, but it makes the point that one cannot tell, when petitions are issued, which marriages are irretrievably broken and which can be helped. It has sometimes been found that the parties who show the greatest hostility towards one another are those who can later come to terms—a finding that would not surprise an experienced marriage counsellor.

In practice, the first and sometimes the only meeting with the counsellor at the conciliation department is nothing more than a screening interview, where the situation is diagnosed by the counsellor. If there does seem to be some point in the parties trying to trace the source of their problems, then they are invited to return for more counselling, or referred to a family service agency, a mental health clinic or to a professional counsellor in private practice.

Under the Wisconsin family code the divorce action is regarded as involving not only the parties and their children, but also the public interest. In the first place, guardians *ad litem* are appointed on behalf of the children of the marriage whenever custody is in dispute, or when there is reason for the court to feel grave concern for their wellbeing. A lawyer is charged in such cases with the duty of acting as the children's representative for the purpose of the divorce action. He receives his fee out of the costs of the action, which are awarded by the judge between the parties at his discretion. Not only is the lawyer appointed to act solely in the interests of the children, but the court also appoints a family court commissioner. This commissioner attends hearings of the divorce action to represent the public interest; his task is related to the investigation already carried out by the counsellor attached to the conciliation department.

Thus, when children are involved there is almost always an additional delay of about three months while an investigation of their present position and their future is made. The court order will provide for their custody and maintenance. It may also direct that arrangements made for the children shall be supervised by the conciliation department, normally for a period of six months or more.

It can be seen that the approach to the problem of family breakdown in Wisconsin is rather different from that adopted in other States. The court, in addition to its other functions, provides a social service to the family in all cases where there are children involved. It holds a watching brief on behalf of the community, and provides individual counselling help for the husband and wife to resolve or alleviate their problems if they wish to take advantage of it.

Wayne County, Michigan. In common with some other States, Michigan recently authorized the establishment of official marriage counselling services. In 1964 the State House of Representatives passed a Marriage Counseling Bill by a large majority, and its provisions, which were permissive, were soon put into effect by the Circuit Court of Wayne County, which contains the city of Detroit. As in other places, professional counsellors are used, and they take part in in-service training projects in conjunction with the University of Detroit and Wayne County University.

The first annual report of the service claimed that two-thirds of the couples who 'completed counseling' found their situations so improved that they abandoned all thought of divorce. The figures are 122 couples out of 186. Apart from those couples who completed counselling, 125 were referred to other community services, and 147 did not return for counselling. The success of the counselling service should therefore be judged in relation to the 458 couples seen, rather than the number who are recorded as having completed counselling. Presumably the 122 who did so represented marriages in which at least one of the parties was ready to consider the prospects of reconciliation. Later annual reports of this court indicate similar figures.

It has been decided to make a charge to all clients using the court marriage counselling service, a provision not found elsewhere. Fees depend on the income of the parties. If the joint income of husband and wife is less than $5,000 (£2,080) there is no fee to pay. In addition, there is exemption given of $600 in respect of each child of the marriage. To give examples, a couple earning $8,000 between them, and with two children, would be charged $4 for each interview; a childless couple earning $11,000 would pay $11; the same fee would be paid by a couple earning £13,400, but with four children.

Most referrals to the court marriage counselling service, as elsewhere in the United States, are made by the legal profession. These amount to nearly 69 per cent of all referrals; almost all the rest are made to the counsellors direct by the court, or from the court's allied services. There is no mandatory procedure. In 60 per cent of all cases the first partner to attend a counsellor was the wife. Husbands came first in 26 per cent of cases, and in the remainder the parties came together. In rather more than half the cases the parties were already separated. Statistical analysis of the court's records shows that in 29 per cent of cases the families involved had two children, 21 per cent had three children, 17 per cent one child and 18 per cent no children. By far the greater number of clients were in the skilled or professional class, the figures for husbands being as follows:

Skilled	39%
Professional, Management	27%
Semi-skilled	25%
Unskilled	6%
Unemployed	1%

| Retired | 1% |
| Unknown | 1% |

The most likely income of couples was in the region of $8,ooo, and so the great majority of clients have to pay fees for the service that they receive.

New York. In March 1966 the New York State Legislature enacted the first major revision of divorce law in the State since the year 1787. It is now possible to obtain a divorce on the grounds of cruel and inhuman treatment by the defendant spouse, also for abandonment of the plaintiff by the defendant for a period of two or more years, for confinement to prison of the defendant for three or more consecutive years, and for adultery. A divorce decree can also be obtained following a decree of judicial separation, if the parties have in fact lived apart for a period of two years or more. Most citizens of the State of New York who wished for a divorce had previously to go to other States, or even to other countries such as Mexico. The old State law had allowed divorce on the grounds of adultery, but had forbidden the remarriage of the guilty party.

The new provisions have brought the law of the State of New York more into line with that of many of the other States in America, but there is one novel provision in the new law that establishes a complicated procedure for marital conciliation. At the expense of the State of New York, a Conciliation Bureau has been set up, and under the supervision of the supreme court a three-stage conciliation process has been established. The three stages are a conciliation conference, followed by counselling and by conciliation hearings.

In each judicial district of the State of New York a conciliation bureau is established, the head of each bureau being one of the justices of the supreme court. The justice has to be appointed as head of the bureau by a majority of the judges of the appellate division of the judicial department for the district. He is entitled the 'supervising justice' and is given power to appoint, 'as many persons as may be necessary to be conciliation commissioners, special guardians and counselors', all of whom will receive a fee for the work they do, paid by the State and not by the parties.

As soon as divorce proceedings have been commenced, the plaintiff is required to file a notice of the action with the conciliation bureau, whereupon the case is assigned by the supervising justice to one of the conciliation commissioners. These commissioners must be lawyers who have had at least five years' practice in New York. The notice to the bureau states the names and ages of the parties and of their children, and also the nature of the proceedings that have been commenced. The notice must be given to the bureau within ten days of the filing of the divorce petition, and within another five days the commissioner may fix a date for a conciliation conference. Both parties must attend this conference with a counsellor, and after hearing what they have to say, the counsellor makes a decision as to whether the case should proceed to the next conciliation stage. It is of course possible for the counsellor to see the parties several times, if they wish, but they can only be compelled to attend one such conference.

The conciliation commissioner may refer the parties to one of the counsellors appointed by the supervising justice, or may alternatively issue a certificate of 'no necessity'. Such a certificate states that it is not necessary for the conciliation process to be continued, and would no doubt be issued when the commissioner came to the conclusion that any attempt in this direction would be useless, for instance in a case where great violence had been used. The obvious danger is that, under the heavy pressure of work, the issue of such certificates might become automatic, for fear that the staff of counsellors should be overwhelmed by too many referrals.

However, if referral for counselling is made by the commissioner it may be to an outside counselling agency or to one of the court counsellors. If one of the parties fails to attend the conciliation conference to which he has been called, he can be compelled to do so under pain of imprisonment for contempt of court. In addition to his power to refer the parties for a conciliation conference in cases where he does not issue a certificate of 'no necessity', the commissioner may also appoint a special guardian to look after the interests of any children who may be involved. When a special guardian is appointed in this way he is regarded as a party to the proceedings in much the same way as a guardian *ad litem* acts in the Milwaukee courts. The special guardians have power to consult with the commissioner, with the parties to the action, and also with any counsellor who has been assigned to the case, and they may make recommendations to the court relating to the custody of the children whose interests they are there to protect. These recommendations are made by way of reports filed with the commissioner, and with the supervising justice.

Conciliation conferences, under the terms of the new law, are required to be 'conducted informally' and they must be held within ten days after the matter has been referred to the counsellor by the commissioner. The law provides that, if the parties to the action consent, the counsellor may refer them for the help of doctors, clergy or psychiatrists. If all these attempts at reconciliation fail, the counsellor then makes a report to the commissioner, whose task is then to hold a conciliation hearing. The counsellor is expected to make a final report within the short period of thirty days of the matter being referred to him. No doubt this provision was made in order that the process of law should not be delayed, but it would in many cases tend to inhibit the counsellor in his work with the client, which he might wish to extend over a longer period than one month. In any event, within twenty days of the report from the counsellor the commissioner has to fix a day for the conciliation hearing.

Conciliation hearings are different from conciliation conferences in that they are conducted more formally. Each party is entitled to be heard, to be represented by his or her own lawyer, and to cross-examine witnesses. Attendance by the parties may be compelled, and witnesses may also be made to attend. Clearly the atmosphere will be very much that of a judicial proceeding, and there has been much criticism of the new law on the grounds that it is likely to increase considerably the cost of divorce proceedings to the parties.

It is open to the commissioner at the hearing to conclude that there are after all no prospects of a reconciliation, but it is equally open to him to find that reconciliation is possible and that it would best serve the interests of husband and wife and of their children. If he makes the latter finding he will then apply for an order from the supervising justice which will require the parties to attempt to effect a reconciliation. Such an attempt at reconciliation cannot be required to extend over a period of more than sixty days. At the end of this period the parties are free to proceed with a divorce.

It is difficult to see what beneficial effect such an order can possibly have. There is no other court in the United States that is empowered to make such an order, and it is the general opinion of those concerned with social work in the New York area that the new law will not permit the existence of the conditions which they feel are essential to promote reconciliation. Fundamentally it is held by these sources that the parties themselves must be free to decide for themselves whether or not they wish to reconcile.[1] It has even been suggested that it may be a violation of the due process of law to require parties to attempt to effect a reconciliation.[2]

The first attempts at reconciliation procedures under the new law of the State of New York have only recently been made, and it is not yet possible to see what effect they will have. Under the law, parties may be prevented from obtaining their desired divorce by as much as 120 days, if the full process of conciliation conference, counsellor's report and conciliation hearing takes place, followed by the mandatory reconciliation order. On the other hand, if the conciliation commissioner issues an immediate 'no necessity' certificate, the divorce need only be delayed by as little as fifteen days.

Utah. In 1957 the State of Utah enacted a Marriage Counseling Law. The service thus established was abolished only four years later, in 1961, but it is instructive to study its operation and the reasons for its abandonment. The law provided, and still provides, for a ninety-day 'cooling off' period between the date on which a divorce petition is filed and the date on which it can first come on for hearing. Either party could request a conciliation conference at which the court had power to compel attendance, and the counsellors were engaged to work throughout the State of Utah. There were eight full-time and four part-time counsellors engaged, salaries ranging from between $415 and $585 per month.

[1] Community Service Society of New York. *Divorce Reform 1967—A Plea to the Legislature.*

[2] Prof Hy. J. Foster Jr. and Dr D. J. Freed, New York, 1967. *The Divorce Reform Law.*

The first major difficulty was that, when the counsellors first began work, there was a large backlog of cases waiting for them. The statute had provided that they should be available not only for conciliation conferences held at the request of the parties, but also to act as domestic relations counsellors, acting as court officials reviewing such matters as child support and custody. The counsellors themselves tended to prefer working with those cases where there seemed the best prospects of reconciliation, and these cases most often arose from voluntary requests from people who were not even involved in litigation. The result of this was that the backlog of cases remained long and that the courts did not feel that the statutory functions of the counsellors in regard to child custody and support were being properly maintained.

It seems that another factor in the breakdown of the plan was the administrative control of the work of the counsellors. They were responsible to the State Department of Welfare, and not to the courts. The welfare department appointed the counsellors and paid their salaries, and their primary loyalty was therefore naturally to that department. It was also the practice in the State of Utah for the judges to undertake only short spells of work in the domestic relations courts, and this reduced the likelihood of a close working relationship between them and the counsellors.

By the time the scheme was abandoned in 1961, a total of 5,883 cases had been referred by the courts to the counsellors, and it was reported that 1,295 (22·1 per cent) of these had resulted in reconciliation. Of 775 referrals made direct to the counsellors and not by the courts, 342 reconciliations (44 per cent) were reported. The plan was beginning to develop as a community service available on a voluntary basis, and indeed was showing signs of successful operation, but because it was not serving its originally intended purpose it was brought to an end.

Other Counselling and Conciliation Services
The Marriage Council of Philadelphia. In Philadelphia there is a Marriage Council, which exists 'to help people to a better understanding of what married life involves and thereby to aid them in achieving a richer and more satisfying relationship'. The Marriage Council is a private and independent organization,

having a close relationship with the University of Philadelphia. It has no formal links with the courts. The staff are professional workers holding graduate degrees, with additional special training in marriage counselling; there are medical and legal supervisory committees. The premises used by the Council are in a pleasant old house, near the main university buildings but some way from the centre of Philadelphia.

The counselling services of the Marriage Council are available to clients singly or together; they are given to those about to marry, those having difficulty in marriage, and those who are considering bringing their marriages to an end. The service is offered in two ways, by private interview and by group discussion, but all clients have at least one preliminary individual interview. After this first interview they are advised on the type of counselling that is thought to be likely to help them most. During an average year 4,000 counselling sessions take place, and 800 clients are helped. In 80 per cent of the cases both husband and wife are seen by a counsellor attached to the Council.

All clients are asked to pay a fee based on their income. For the first interview the comparatively high fee of $25 is charged for a married couple, or $15 for one individual. The client arranges the amount of subsequent fees with the counsellor, but not less than $10 is charged for each session. The cost of group counselling works out at not less than $15 for each couple attending. These fees are paid to the Council, and not to the counsellor, who receives his salary direct from the Council.

Clients' payments make up approximately 19 per cent of the Council's income. The major part of its income is from a grant provided by the National Institute for Mental Health, but substantial sums are also received from foundations interested in research projects, from training fees for graduate study and from members' subscriptions. These subscriptions are from the general public and represent 10 per cent of the Council's income. Contributions from these members range from $5 a year to $50 or more, and there are five classes of membership. Every member of the Council is entitled to one vote at general meetings. The business of the Council is managed from year to year by a board of trustees, who hold office for three years. The board appoints a president of the Council, also a vice-president, secretary and treasurer. The constitution of the Council provides that the president shall be the chief executive officer of the Council. He presides at meetings of the board and of the Council. The board of trustees also appoint an executive director whose job is to carry on the day-to-day work of the Council, and to appoint and supervise staff members.

These constitutional provisions indicate a somewhat different set-up from other counselling organizations in the United States. There is no link with the judicial system, but instead a close contact with the university. All staff members work on lines provided in a detailed *Office Manual* issued by the Marriage Council, which covers such matters as hours of work, allowances for meals, holidays and sick leave. It also sets out the terms of appointment of staff members, and makes provision for regular checks on the quality of the work. This evaluation is made under six headings:

Quality of job performance
Quality of job organization
Ability to maintain co-operative work relationship
Rate of progress
Evaluation of professional staff
Additional interests.

This very detailed assessment procedure is used not only to supervise staff members, but also for the support of students taking the graduate training course in association with the university. Those who have completed this training course now hold positions in thirty States in the USA and in other parts of the world. The Marriage Council also provides training in similar work for clergy and also navy chaplains.

Beyond the general service to the public, and the training programme, the Marriage Council conducts, in association with the university, research which is designed to promote the understanding of conflicts between married people, the process and outcome of marriage counselling and the factors making for success in family life. This very ambitious programme of research is supported by private foundations and by federal and state grants. A large library is maintained, and members of the staff have published many books and articles. The work of the

Marriage Council of Philadelphia is well known both in America and in other parts of the world.

The Council has a clearly defined policy regarding the outside employment of its staff. There are no restrictions on part-time members taking up other paid work, but full-time members do not normally accept remuneration from other sources, for instance private practice. Private work that is undertaken by staff members, whether full-time or part-time, is expected to be to the professional standards established by the Council. The Council is not only steadily increasing its work in marriage counselling but is also becoming more active in family life education. At present this is done mostly with pre-marital groups, so the majority of these clients are close to marriage. Present plans envisage a considerable expansion of this aspect of the Marriage Council's work.

American Institute for Family Relations. This institute is situated in California, and provides a marriage counselling service. It is based on the city of Los Angeles, and its work first began in 1930. It claims that it has developed from the first organized attempt in the USA to bring the resources of modern science to aid the promotion of marriage and successful family life. The institute does not exist to make a profit, and it is employing over twenty marriage counsellors who are licensed to practise by Californian State law. It also employs medical and other staff. Counselling is given to married couples, and to a wide range of other people; it takes place individually and in groups.

The institute also gives training in marriage counselling, and runs a summer workshop on the techniques of marriage and family counselling. Since its formation the institute states that it has trained more marriage counsellors than any other organization in the United States; candidates are required to have a degree before they start the course, which lasts six months or more. The course commences with a study of cases and with reading, attendance at lectures and later 'multiple counselling', which involves sitting with an experienced counsellor who is dealing with an appropriate client. Several trainee counsellors may attend this multiple training session. Counsellors pay a registration fee of $100 for the course, but after some time they can expect to receive an honorarium for the work they are doing at the institute. The summer workshop run by the institute costs each participant $75 and lasts a fortnight. Mornings are devoted to lectures and discussions, while afternoons are taken up with work in smaller groups.

The American Institute for Family Relations has a comprehensive list of publications, and special courses for members of the general public. Among many others, there are courses entitled *Helping People with their Problems* designed for men and women who wish to help churches or other community organizations dealing with clients needing assistance. The normal fee for joining this course is $20 a month, meetings being held weekly. A similar fee is charged for other courses, and these are provided for expectant mothers, for women seeking improved sexual adjustment with their husbands, and for others. The institute publishes a regular monthly journal entitled *Family Life*.

Fees charged for marriage counselling at the institute are normally $10 an hour, though special arrangements can be made for clients who are unable to pay. They obtain their counselling in such cases through the institute's training programme, which means that they will be seen by a counsellor in training rather than by the permanent staff of the institute. Also, they may be helped during one of the 'multiple counselling' sessions mentioned above.

Some clients come to the institute for help from other parts of America, and as they may only be able to stay for a comparatively short time they may need a more intensive form of help than the normal pattern of weekly counselling interviews. These clients can be given 'concentrated' counselling consisting of four, six or even sometimes eight hours' counselling a day, over several consecutive days. As these counselling sessions involve some disruption of the normal programme of the institute, a higher charge is made, the fee varying between $15 and $20 per hour. Finally, some clients are charged $20 per month for regular attendance at weekly group counselling sessions, each of which lasts one and a half hours.

North Carolina. At Black Mountain, North Carolina, a Counselling and Consultation Service is operated under the sponsorship of the Protestant Episcopal Church. It is a good example of a marriage conciliation service provided by a church, and the senior counsellor at Black Mountain is Ralph Bridgman, formerly associated with the family court at Toledo, Ohio. The service helps people in marital difficulty, and is also acting as a centre for the training of clergy in pastoral counselling. In addition to marriage counselling, group counselling is provided for young people, and lectures, retreats and seminars are held. Counselling sessions take place at the Episcopal centre in Black Mountain, and the service is described as 'an expression of the Church's responsibility to the community'.

The counselling service supplements the work of the parishes and provides 'a religion-oriented referral resource' for doctors, lawyers and others. Members of the clergy in the locality can consult the service concerning their parishioners who are having marriage problems. Some clients come direct to the service, and they will be seen separately or together, as suits them best. Sessions are private and confidential, and reports are not made to any other person without permission of the client. Between three and four counselling sessions are held on each working day by the counsellor employed by the service.

The service is financed partly from the fees that the clients pay, and partly from contributions from the Diocese of Western North Carolina of the Protestant Episcopal Church. The fee that the client is to pay is agreed between him and the counsellor at the first session, and the service makes the point that the larger fees paid by some of its clients enable help to be given to others who cannot afford to pay so much. In the first two years of the operation of the service it was found that 85 per cent of the agreed fees had in fact been collected. A professional advisory committee exists to advise the service on policy matters, its members including doctors, psychologists and social workers. The Committee meets twice a year, and has some twenty members.

The Oklahoma City Family Clinic. A most unusual form of marriage conciliation service exists in Oklahoma City, known as the Oklahoma City Family Clinic. Clients are charged no fee, although they are expected to make a small donation towards the cost of maintaining the service, which is staffed almost entirely voluntarily.

The clients of the clinic are seen by a panel of four people, comprised of one physician, one minister, one businessman and one lawyer. From these professions in Oklahoma City a large number of men and women give their time voluntarily, members of the panels serving in rotation so as to divide the work between them. No conference with clients is held unless all four members of the panel are present.

The initiative in setting up the Oklahoma City Family Clinic was taken by a lawyer, Mr Bliss Kelly, and in 1947 his plan was presented to a meeting of the Oklahoma City Council of Churches for approval. The council of churches, having set up a committee to consider the plan, gave its support, but took no further action because it wished to avoid any appearance that the clinic might seem solely to be a church-inspired group. The main reason for this decision was that most people seeking a divorce are not regular church-goers. The plan was also approved by the professional associations, the County Bar Association, the County Medical Society and the Retail Merchants Association. Each association names about twenty-five people from whom the selection for the panels is regularly made, and brief reports of the clinic's work are made each year to the association.

Meetings of the panels are held at such places as the Red Cross premises, the Young Men's Christian Association building, and the Variety Club Health Centre in Oklahoma City. Offices of professional people are not used, the object being to provide a neutral meeting place. A secretary to the clinic is essential, and when it was first set up a woman was appointed to this post. She attends all hearings of the panel. Her task is to take details of essential facts brought out during the lengthy session with the clients, to note the recommendations made by the panel, and to follow up these recommendations. The growth of the work of the clinic has been such that there is now one secretary to arrange appointments, and another six serving as 'follow-up secretaries'.

The clinic states that it is a most important rule that plenty of time must always be allotted for the hearing of each case. No member of the panel must be anxious to leave for another appointment, and three to four hours are allowed for the couple seeking help to talk, and to listen to the advice given to them. Panel members are expected to be patient and to hear the full story from each party, asking questions as and when necessary. The view is that without this procedure proper recommendations cannot be made.

Before they have come to meet the panel, the couple who have asked for its help with their marriage problems have completed a detailed questionnaire, and have signed a form entitled 'consent to attempt changes'. The questionnaire states that an appointment has been fixed for both husband and wife to attend; they are requested not to bring their children, but to arrange for their care at home. 'Both parties', continues the questionnaire, 'must be willing to make a sincere effort to follow the recommendations made. This means a willingness to change many ideas and habits and "do an about-face" when necessary. It is also important that reports be made weekly and monthly to the secretary as long as necessary so that progress may be aided and additional assistance given when needed.'

The questionnaire seeks general details of the couple, their occupations, education, past illnesses and other matters, including a short statement of their views on the root cause of the trouble. This questionnaire has already been read by all members of the panel before the hearing, which always takes place in a private room. In the room are a table and seven chairs, two of which are at one end of the table, where husband and wife sit; the other chairs are for the panel members and the secretary. The secretary has a copy of the well-known book *How to Win Friends and Influence People* by Dale Carnegie, a family budget book, and a paper-weight stone, which at this stage is turned away from the couple.

When the couple come in they sit at the two chairs at the end of the table, and are addressed by the chairman, usually the lawyer on the panel, who is known as the moderator. He explains the procedure to them, promising that everything they say is absolutely confidential but explaining that they must promise to tell the panel everything, good or bad, which might have a bearing on their trouble. 'This is very important,' he says, 'for if you are not willing to tell us everything we cannot help you and we may as well go home now. If something has happened in the past life of either of you which you agreed not to tell, then you must change before we go ahead, as we would give you wrong advice.' The moderator goes on to explain that each is to be asked to tell his story in turn, and that while this is going on the other must under no circumstances interrupt. Each has a pencil and paper, and any points on which one wishes to comment are to be noted while the other is talking, to be brought up later.

The moderator points out that the panel is not there to allot blame, but to help them both. This adds point to the provision of pencil and paper, for the couple are expected to write down any recommendations made by the panel. He seeks their assurance that they will try to follow the recommendations made, and insists that they answer positively. He concludes with some such words as these:

'We will try to be good listeners. The doctor will not try to cure you today, the minister will not try to save your soul today and the financier will not try to pull you out of debt this afternoon, but we will try to show you how to do these things, with help, for yourselves. We will make notes as you talk, but just go right ahead with your stories. It is immaterial which talks first—one of you start in and tell us what's on your mind.'

The first speaker then tells his or her story. If he seems to wander into recriminations, the moderator tries to bring him back to the story. When it is finished, each member of the panel asks questions relating to his particular field, as well as anything less pertinent. No recommendations are made at this stage, for the other partner has not yet told his side of the story. When the first process is complete, the other spouse is asked to tell his or her version of what has happened. Plenty of time is taken, and the session is never hurried. The clinic finds that it is often apparent that one or both of the parties has to be examined in detail to persuade him to bring out matters that are being covered up. They are expected, as the Oklahoma clinic puts it, 'to scrape the bottom of the barrel'.

At the end of this lengthy process the panel members make their recommendations, the minister speaking last. Many specific recommendations are made, but each member admits that these are only superficial and that the real task is for husband and wife to stop trying to change one another, but instead to make attempts to change themselves. At the end of the recommendations they are asked if they have prayed about their problems. The names of the panel members are then given to the couple with the request that they make contact with each as the need arises. Appointments are made for financial conferences with the businessman, and for a series of thirty-minute talks with the minister over a period of four to six weeks, also with the doctor and lawyer as necessary. The Dale Carnegie book is given to them with the suggestion that they study it carefully and use its formulas on each other. In appropriate cases they are given the budget book, and then the paper-weight stone is turned round so that the inscription on it faces them. On the stone are the words 'The first stone; let him who is without sin cast it'. The conference closes with a prayer, the couple holding hands.

This whole procedure is so very different from any other in the United States, or indeed in the rest of the world, that some further description is necessary. The clinic confirms that the question often arises as to how their scheme can operate effectively without the use of trained counsellors on family problems. The answer, they say, is simple, for the family counsellor only hears one side of the story, and does not have available the advice of four professional people. They add that there will always be a shortage of trained counsellors for those marriages where only one party can be persuaded to come for help.

At an early stage the founders of the clinic thought that they would be very fortunate if they succeeded in effecting 50 per cent reconciliations of those couples who came for their help. In fact, they are claiming that between 80 and 90 per cent of these couples establish happy homes. This is in spite of the fact, they say, that most of the cases were aggravated, had what appeared to be insurmountable difficulties, and were highly involved and difficult of solution. In 10 per cent of the cases there had already been a divorce of the couple concerned, and in another 23 per cent of cases divorce suits were pending. The clinic had also been asked why no use of social workers, psychiatrists, psychologists and others has been made. Their reply is that the problems of human life come within the professional fields covered by the four members of the panel, and that if other specialists are needed then they are called in, or the couple is sent to them. The clinic say that at the conferences couples will tell intimate facts that they often cannot bring themselves to tell in private to their own professional advisers. It is invariably found that one spouse speaks of some cause of complaint that he has never before mentioned to the other.

It is quite clear that, although efforts are made to avoid an obvious association with the church, the method of working employed by the panels clearly implies a religious belief. The minister usually follows up the hearing with a personal call on the couple within a week or two. Panel members and the organizers of the clinic say that they are approached frequently by 'quacks, crackpots and do-gooders' and that such persons have to be brushed off. The clinic has no connection with the Community Welfare Services, as they say that many couples would not come to them if there was such a link.

It has been explained that the secretary is present at all conferences. She takes notes of all recommendations of the panel, and it is part of her job to follow up each couple, checking at frequent intervals to find out whether they are carrying out the recommendations made to them. She may arrange for additional conferences with the whole panel or with its individual members. The summary of the clinic's work states that 'in many cases two to ten months is required for the couple to attain full compliance with the recommendations made'. Clients often need a reminder to help them to make a start, and very few of them apparently begin to take action within the first month after the meeting with the panel. That many of them do then begin to take some action is clearly due to the considerable 'follow-up' work done by the secretary and by members of the panel. In most cases the couple have conferences with at least two panel members after the hearing, and often with all four of them.

In appointing the secretaries, the clinic does not look for trained people. They are seeking 'sincere, mature women who want to be of service to others without being dictatorial, willing to listen without being upset by what is being said, pleasantly insistent upon making changes recommended, and wanting only to be of service to others without fee or monetary reward'. Both the secretary and the panel members must be strangers to the couple who have come for their advice. Where similar family clinics have been formed in other areas, cases are often exchanged between one town and another to ensure that the couple are not known to anyone on the panel.

The clinic does not produce annual reports, nor does it make detailed records of work done, for there is no salaried staff to do this. Conferences are held with 150 to 200 couples a year, and these clients are sent to the clinic by judges, lawyers, doctors, employers, ministers and former clients of the clinic. Some clients are sent by members of their own family, who have heard of the clinic's work. The majority, however, come as a result of looking through the telephone directory and finding the number of the family clinic. When they do this, they are asked if they will conform to the requirements of the clinic before they are passed on to the appointments secretary. They do so, and are given an appointment on a day at about 1 p.m., which enables the session to go on until 5 p.m. or later. If the necessary probing has not been completed, and all parties are exhausted after many hours of conversation, a second conference is fixed. 'In the ordinary conference,' the clinic's summary states, 'the couple will be stimulated by the long session but the panellists will be worn out, trying to keep their thinking ahead of the couple and come up with the right recommendations.' As the panel members are busy people, appointments are made some weeks in advance of the hearing, and the couple are told to 'hold everything' until a conference can be arranged.

Those responsible for running the Oklahoma Family Clinic consider that they are running a 'pilot plant'. They say that what is next needed is to put the plan into effect in the legal system of other States. They claim also that the effect on the community of the provision of their marriage conciliation service has been considerable. They point to the fact that, although the population of Oklahoma City has doubled since they began their work, the number of divorces has remained constant.

Similar clinics are being established in other parts of the USA, almost all of them taking their pattern from the Oklahoma Clinic. One such clinic is at Salem, Oregon. A similar fee is charged there as to clients in Oklahoma, the clinic being run by the local Young Men's Christian Association. It is called the Salem Marriage Clinic. Couples are asked to sign a 'consent slip' by which they agree to follow the recommendations made to them. On the back of the slip is a list of all the lawyers, doctors, ministers, businessmen and secretaries normally in attendance at the clinic, so that the couple can indicate those who are already personally known to them.

At Salem, the panel members write out their recommendations on a sheet of paper; they are not expected to limit these to their own particular field but 'each counsellor should give of the personal knowledge and experience, the ideas and ideals he has gained as a husband and father'. As in Oklahoma, there is stress on spiritual values; the panel members normally pray together before the hearing commences. Meetings are usually held in the late afternoons rather than at 1 p.m., so they normally continue late into the evening. The Salem Clinic has been operating since 1957, and in its first eight years saw 325 couples, an average of forty couples a year. There are some forms of orientation provided for panel members, but this does not amount to systematic training in marriage counselling work.

This brief account of the services at Oklahoma City and at Salem illustrates the considerable diversity of approaches to marital conciliation in the United States. It is to be doubted whether many trained social workers would see much value in these procedures, in spite of the fact that men and women with a certain amount of professional training take part in them.

Chapter 9

UNITED STATES OF AMERICA
—CONCILIATION COURTS

The Conciliation Courts
Los Angeles. In 1939, the State of California passed legislation enabling counties within the State to establish conciliation courts and to provide them with full-time staff. The county of Los Angeles set up such a court in the same year, but it was not greeted with enthusiasm either by the judges or by the practising lawyers, and an unsuccessful attempt was made after only two years to abolish the conciliation court altogether. The court made little progress during its first fifteen years of life; as late as 1954 it was employing no professionally trained marriage counsellors, but in that year Judge Louis H. Burke was appointed presiding judge of the court. Judge Burke was responsible for instituting legislation to give the court the financial means to begin effective work.

Some attempt to arrest the rising tide of divorce was certainly due; in 1955, some 28,500 actions were started in the Los Angeles courts involving the domestic affairs of the parties. Over 33,000 young children were involved in these marriages. In the United States as a whole, there is one divorce for every four marriages, and in the case of marriages contracted when both partners are under twenty, there is one divorce for every two such marriages. Over half the divorces granted are to couples with at least one child under the age of eighteen.

Judge Burke had come to the conclusion that only by the use of professionally trained counsellors could the conciliation court hope to make any impact on the increasing number of divorce cases. It is the present court's view that 'Wherever unqualified and inexperienced personnel have been used, or an untrained judge has been assigned to perform such services, the conciliation processes have universally failed, and the entire programme criticized by attorneys, the judiciary, and the general public'.

The legal provisions for the existence and operation of the conciliation court are contained in the California Code of Civil Procedure, in Sections 1730 to 1772, the object of the legislation being stated as 'to provide means for the reconciliation of spouses and the amicable settlement of domestic and family controversies'. Every superior court in California is given power to establish a conciliation court, and specific provision is made for the remuneration of the counsellors attached to the courts. The code declares that no fees are to be charged for the filing of petitions, or for the services of the counsellors attached to the court.

Section 1747 of the code relates to the privileged nature of conferences, hearings and communications involved in the operation of the court. Only the officers of the court, the parties, their lawyers and any necessary witnesses are permitted to attend. The section continues: 'The files of the conciliation court shall be closed. The petition, supporting affidavit, reconciliation agreement and any court order made in the matter may be opened to inspection to any party or his counsel upon the written authority of the judge of the conciliation court.' The effect of this section is to ensure that all the work of the counsellors attached to the court is confidential. It is a universal view that husbands and wives are less likely to confide in a counsellor if they fear that what they say may be repeated. The only documents, in fact, to which even the parties and their lawyers have access are the husband and wife agreement, to which reference will be made later, and the legal documents that have to be lodged with the court when the conciliation petition is filed.

Conciliation petitions may be filed, under the provisions of Section 1761, 'for the purpose of effecting a reconciliation between the parties, or for amicable settlement of the controversy between the spouses, so as to avoid further litigation over the issue involved'. This section is designed not only to cover the attempt to resolve the difficulties that have arisen in the marriage, but also to enable the husband and wife to discuss such questions as the custody of children. It has been found in California, as elsewhere, that even where reconciliation is impossible it is still worth while trying to reach agreement on matters of custody, maintenance and the ownership of property. This can save expense, and is particularly helpful where there

L   161

are children involved, because bitter litigation can only result in harm to them.

If a divorce is to be granted to a couple with a family it is surely in their own interest, and that of their children, that arrangements for the future should be made calmly and without unnecessary suffering. Such a provision can in fact save considerable time and expense, because contested proceedings relating, for example, to a father's access to his children will involve the preparation of the case by the lawyers, the time of the court, and all the fees that this entails. If the counsellor can help the couple resolve these practical problems together, the solution is likely to be far more acceptable and workable than would be the case if the court had to impose a solution.

Section 1769 states that any reconciliation agreement between the parties may be reduced to writing and a court order may be made, provided both parties consent, requiring them to comply with its terms. The court is given power to make orders relating to the conduct of husband and wife, so far as is necessary to preserve the marriage or to implement the reconciliation, but orders made under this power are only effective for thirty days following the hearing of the petition, unless the parties together consent to an extension of this period. The court uses this power to order, for instance, that the parties shall keep to the terms of a reconciliation agreement, or to prevent a third person from interfering between husband and wife. It would be almost impossible to enforce any such orders for any length of time, as they essentially depend on the continuing willingness of the parties to abide by them; hence the time limit of thirty days on the effectiveness of the orders, giving them a short period of time in which to work.

The code gives the conciliation court jurisdiction in all cases where there is a child of the marriage who is still a minor. Where there is no such child the court has power to assume jurisdiction where the prospects of reconciliation seem reasonably good.

Any married couple living in the county of Los Angeles can start proceedings in the conciliation court, whether or not a divorce petition has been filed. The person filing the petition, as it is called, does not necessarily have to employ a lawyer to do this, but merely completes a form headed 'Petition for Conciliation'. The form is designed to show details of the spouses, their addresses and telephone numbers, the number and names of their children, and ends with the following words:

'Your Petitioner therefore prays that this honorable court will make such orders in respect to the conduct of the spouses and the subject matter of the controversy as the court deems necessary to preserve the marriage, or effect a reconciliation of the spouses, or an amicable settlement of the controversies involved.

'I certify that the Petition is made in good faith and with the hope of effecting a reconciliation; that I promise to do nothing to prejudice these proceedings during the pendency of the Petition and for thirty (30) days hereafter; that during this period I will not conceal, divert or dispose of any assets to which my spouse has or claims to have any interest therein, under penalty of contempt.'

On filing this petition the spouse seeking reconciliation is then sent a form of declaration which is designed to show the problems that have occurred in the marriage. The form asks for information first about the employment of the spouses, their state of health, and for details of any previous divorces of either party. The form then continues:

'A check list of problems is provided for your use. Please indicate below what you feel the problems to be and further comments if you wish. (Indicate "Yes" by check mark.)
Financial problems ( )
Unfaithfulness; by husband ( ) by wife ( )
Bad temper; of husband ( ) of wife ( )
In-law problems ( )
Sexual problems ( )
Nagging; by husband ( ) by wife ( )
Excessive use of liquor; by husband ( ) by wife ( )
Lack of communication (unable to talk over problems);
    by husband ( ) by wife ( )
Selfish, childish or irresponsible behaviour;
    by husband ( ) by wife ( )
Lack of mutual social life ( )
Lack of family friends ( )

Excessive absence from home; by husband (   ) by wife (   )
Physical abuse; by husband to wife (   ) by wife to
    husband (   )
Disagreements about raising the children (   )
Jealousy; by husband (   ) by wife (   )
Ill health; of husband (   ) of wife (   )
Loss of trust; by husband (   ) by wife (   )
Loss of respect; by husband (   ) by wife (   )
Loss of affection; by husband (   ) by wife (   )
Religious conflict (   )
Late hours; by husband (   ) by wife (   )
Extreme dependency on parents; by husband (   ) by wife (   )
Gambling; by husband (   ) by wife (   )
Domineering; by husband (   ) by wife (   )

Comment on further problems here ....
....

    This form is passed to the counsellor who has been assigned to the case, and both husband and wife receive a letter from the presiding judge, requesting them to attend at the court's offices on a stated day. The respondent, that is the spouse who did not file the petition, is told 'We trust you will keep this appointment voluntarily and avoid the necessity of requiring the court to issue a subpoena'. The court's view is that this 'gentle judicial coercion' plays an important part in effecting reconciliations, because some partners, though secretly hoping to mend the marriage, feel that to take the first steps towards a reconciliation would involve a loss of face. One counsellor attached to the court sees the letter as a 'catalytic agent' which enables the couple to sit down and discuss their problems together.

    If divorce proceedings have already been started, the filing of a conciliation petition does not prevent them from going forward. Originally the filing of a petition had the effect of staying all proceedings for a month, but many spouses began to use the conciliation procedure as a delaying action, which tended to reduce the value of the court's work. Now, if a petition is filed before divorce proceedings have started, such proceedings must be delayed by at least thirty days, thus giving the counsellor an opportunity to see both the husband and the wife. The court's jurisdiction only extends for thirty days after the petition has been filed, unless the husband and wife consent to its continuance.

At first, most conciliation petitions were filed by husbands, probably because the majority of divorce actions were started by wives. At the present time petitions are equally divided between husbands and wives; this change is ascribed to the introduction of a leaflet, A *Personal Message to Parents,* which is described later in this chapter. It is not necessary for the spouse who seeks a reconciliation to file a petition through a lawyer; it is possible for clients to walk in off the street, and to see a counsellor at short notice. Arrangements are made at the conciliation court to enable this to be done, because the official view is that the problems facing these people are often most urgent, and that delay can result in an unnecessary divorce. The court charges no fees for any of its conciliation services.

At the appointed time the spouses arrive at the conciliation court building, and together see the counsellor for what is known as a 'joint conciliation conference'. This is quite a brief meeting, during which the counsellor describes the counselling process, its purpose and nature. Following this, he sees each partner separately, and while one partner is being interviewed the other is asked to read the 'Husband and Wife Agreement', or Reconciliation Agreement. During the individual interviews the counsellor tries to discover the areas of difficulty in the marriage and why, if at all, one partner wants to save it. He is helped in this by the checklist previously described, and by the client's own comments.

Later on there is a two-hour joint conciliation conference, which the court describes as 'an effective medium for short-term marital counselling'. The counsellor has the opportunity to see for himself the conflict that is going on between husband and wife. His function is to help them see what has been happening in their marriage. This conciliation conference sometimes ends in deadlock, or failure; the couple may decide that there is no purpose in making further attempts at a reconciliation, in which case the counsellor's work is at an end. However, some husbands and wives do come to the conclusion that it is in fact possible to try to re-establish their marriages, and they are then encouraged to work out the terms of a reconciliation agreement. This is in effect a form of marriage contract, and is based on the husband and wife agreement already referred to.

The husband and wife agreement is a fairly lengthy document. It starts with the statement that the court's aid has been sought, that a conference has been held, and that it has been agreed that a certain form of conduct will be necessary to preserve the marriage. The spouses sign the agreement, which can contain some sixty paragraphs dealing with the marriage relationship. The agreement goes into considerable detail, even setting out the occasions on which the parties are to go out together in the evening. There is provision for one party admitting having 'nagged' the other, and details can be included governing the amount of household expenses and pocket money that husband and wife are to be allowed out of the joint family income. The sexual relationship is mentioned, also the importance of parents' conduct towards their children, and there is a section where suggestions of family prayers are made. The agreement having been settled, it is finally signed by husband and wife, and also by the counsellor.

No counselling agency other than the Los Angeles conciliation court, and a few similar courts mostly in the State of California, uses an agreement of this kind. Nevertheless, the court claims that it is highly successful; many couples, it is said, write that they have read and re-read the agreement many times following their reconciliation. A psychiatrist has stated that in his opinion the agreement is 'entirely in keeping with the most advanced thinking in the psychiatric field'. One of the counsellors attached to the court has written that the agreement could be 'a source of support for the partner who wants a reconciliation, but who needs assurance that the spouse will make a sincere effort to change his destructive behaviour. This reassurance is particularly important when the problems are those of physical abuse, non-support, or infidelity. Moreover, the agreement represents a form of external control over the partners when the marriage is failing and they are unable to deal with their problems.'

Couples may return to the court to see a counsellor after the agreement has been signed, but they do not often do this. When they do, it is usually to obtain an interpretation of the agreement, or to amend it because of changed circumstances. On the signing of the agreement the work of the counsellor, therefore, is normally at an end, but the conciliation court recognizes that there are occasions when the parties may need continued counselling for a longer period than the three conferences normally offered by the court. When this is the case, the counsellor refers the husband and wife to another counselling agency. The court sends to this agency some short details of the couple, together with a reply-paid card on which the agency indicates whether the couple in fact made use of their services. Most of these agencies are voluntary organizations of the kind whose work has been described in Chapter 8.

The agencies to which the court refers clients normally give priority to them, because it is felt that a period of extended waiting could undo the progress so far made. Two-thirds of the court's clientele, reports one of the counsellors, have problems of a psychological nature that require prolonged treatment, and if the couple will not accept long-term counselling the chances of a reconciliation are much reduced. In some cases, even where the counsellor attached to the court has not been able to help a husband and wife towards a reconciliation, he may refer them to one of these agencies for individual help. There is no suggestion that the court and the agencies compete with one another in any way; they are in fact felt to be complementary.

The signature of the husband and wife agreement is not the end of the reconciliation procedure. It is normally followed by the making of a court order which first states the fact that the agreement has been signed, and then goes on to order the parties to comply with its terms. It is quite normal for the judge to issue the order while interviewing the husband and wife together, shortly after they have signed the agreement. It is his usual practice to congratulate them on their wisdom, and he follows the interview by sending them a letter which makes the point that the marriage that has survived difficulties is always the stronger for having overcome them. The letter also offers further help if difficulties arise again, and informs the parties that they are always free to return for a further interview with the counsellor. Counsellors are not permitted by the court, however, to undertake private counselling; it is the court's opinion that this would impose too great a strain on them. In fact, counsellors are not normally required to take on more than four cases a day.

The counsellors themselves have to have had at least ten years' counselling experience before appointment, and to have acquired a master's degree in the behavioural sciences. The reason for the demand for these qualifications lies in the short-term nature of the counselling. Seeing the spouses a maximum of four times, the counsellor needs to exercise considerable skill in bringing them to a reconciliation. In addition to the qualifications and experience needed, the court feels that it is equally important to have a counsellor with a warm, outgoing personality who can, in the very short time available, form a satisfactory relationship with the client. Counsellors are paid on a salary scale ranging from $9,564 (£4,000) to $11,904 (£4,960), but no charge is made to clients for the service provided by the court.

Referrals to the conciliation court come from several sources: by far the largest source is the legal profession itself, and over half the petitions filed in the court represent referrals by lawyers. This is a considerable tribute to the relationship that exists between the profession and the court, and is due to the fact that the court has always been particularly careful to preserve a good relationship with the legal profession. In former years, many lawyers were reluctant to make referrals, partly because of a feeling that the conciliation court was meddling in their cases. Another cause of difficulty may have been that the work of the conciliation court would have an adverse effect on the attorney's fees. However, the court has made strenuous efforts to win over the legal profession, and in large measure has clearly succeeded. The court has announced its policy in relation to the attorney's fees; these may be awarded to the lawyer in any case that comes before the court, to cover his work in preparing the legal proceedings that have so far taken place.

It seems, moreover, that clients who have been reconciled are either more able or more willing to pay the lawyer's fees. A prominent lawyer in Los Angeles has said that the attorney has a better chance of collecting his fee from a reconciled couple than from a husband who is having to pay money to his wife and children under a court order. He goes on to say that the reconciled couple remain clients of the lawyer for a long time to come, and that in any event if the reconciliation attempt fails the couple normally go back to the same lawyer. Most lawyers in Los Angeles, it is suggested, are concerned to preserve marriages rather than to bring them to an end, as is clear from the number of referrals they make to the court. These referrals have increased in recent years.

The court makes a point of keeping lawyers fully informed of the progress of the conciliation procedure: a letter is sent to both parties' lawyers when the conciliation petition is filed, and also when the husband and wife agreement is signed. The contact goes even further: if a lawyer appears in court and tells the judge that the husband and wife have in fact reconciled before the case came on for hearing he is urged by the judge to write his clients a letter in the following terms, suggesting that they should avail themselves of the services of the conciliation court to cement the reconciliation:

Dear Mr and Mrs ——,

When I appeared in Court on ...., I stated that you had reconciled. The Judge was very pleased to learn of this. In such cases, however, there are certain formalities which he desires to have you comply with in a final disposition of the matter which, from his long experience, he has concluded would be to your benefit and insure a permanent reconciliation.

With this in mind, he continued the case and ordered *both* of you to appear in Department 8, which is located at 111 North Hill Street, Los Angeles, California, in the County Courts Building, on .... at the hour of .... Do not fail to appear at that time because it is a Court Order.

I have requested the Judge to make an Order allowing me the sum of $...... for my services in this case assuming, of course, that you comply with the Court Order and that the matter is completed in the manner indicated above.

Sincerely yours,

The reason for this procedure, making both husband and wife attend the conciliation court even when they say they have already reconciled, is that the court considers that there is a much better chance of their still being together a year later if they have seen a counsellor and signed the husband and wife agreement. This view is made clear to the parties' lawyer when court writes to him with the draft letter set out above. The court will not in fact allow the parties themselves to bring the case to an end; once the matter has come before the court it ensures that its conciliation services are used, and this it achieves by means of a court order. It will be noted that the reference in the draft letter to fees is designed to ensure that the lawyer receives payment from his client, there being a clear implication that the court has given official sanction to them.

Another 25 per cent of the referrals to the conciliation court come from judges and commissioners associated with other courts in Los Angeles County; the court reports that over half of the couples referred in this way do in fact make application to the conciliation court and are seen by a counsellor. Another major source of referral is a leaflet prepared by the court, bearing the title A Personal Message to Parents. It is sent out to all couples who file divorce petitions and who have at least one child under the age of fourteen. It accounts for most of the remaining applications to the court, and is quite short, starting with the words 'The two minutes you take to read this may change the course of your life. What is said here is not to criticize or blame you for having marital difficulties. These are common to many marriages. This letter suggests a solution which thousands have followed successfully. It is one that is open to you. It costs nothing. It requires only goodwill, some effort, and a sincere desire to do what is best for your children.'

The leaflet goes on to stress the importance of the children in the marriage, and the expense of having to maintain two households, two arguments likely to appeal to most parents of young children. The difficulties and dangers of a second marriage are underlined, and the couple are invited to seek the help of the conciliation court. 'Failure,' it continues, 'is not a popular American word, yet every divorce statistic means two people have failed in life's most noble and important relationship— failed themselves, failed each other, failed their children, failed their Creator, and failed Society. Because our experience proves that most unhappy marriages are merely sick and can be made healthy and happy again, we don't want your marriage to be just another failure.'

It is stressed that the whole conciliation procedure is absolutely confidential; in Los Angeles, in fact, this secrecy is preserved by law, and no files of the court are available to the public. The reader is told that coercion is not used, presumably because most litigants will assume that a message from the court implies the enforcement of an order, and is assured that trained marriage counsellors are available to help the husband and wife, without payment of any fee. On the front of the leaflet is a drawing of an unhappy couple glaring at one another, and of their two anxious children; at the end is another drawing, this time of the reconciled couple, with cheerful children and the message 'This could be you'. The leaflet finishes with an excerpt from a letter sent to the court by a successfully reconciled husband and wife.

Referrals to the conciliation court are also made by the clergy, doctors and other professional people, also by the Bureau of Public Assistance and other organizations, in particular the family service agencies. One of the main reasons why the agencies make referrals, the court reports, is that they have no power to force unwilling spouses to attend a conciliation conference, a power which the court does possess. This brings us to the use of the court's authority, and to the position of the presiding judge.

Once the husband and wife agreement has been signed by both parties, and counter-signed by the judge, it then has the effect of an order of the court, and if either party then breaks its terms they can be punished for contempt of court. The effect of this sanction naturally depends on the use made of it. The court regards it as 'more in the nature of a psychological weapon rather than a force to be actually used'. In other words, it is used but rarely—but it is used. On at least one occasion a husband and his mistress broke one of the terms of the agreement, no doubt a clause preventing them from associating with one another, and both were sentenced to a short term of imprisonment as a punishment for contempt of court.

The counsellor, if the respondent declines to attend for an interview, can recommend to the judge that a subpoena be issued, or alternatively that the conciliation proceedings be brought to an end. Normally, the judge acts on the counsellor's advice, and may order the reluctant husband or wife to appear at the conciliation court on a named day and at a certain time. The court thinks that this power to enforce attendance is extremely valuable. Often enough one of the partners, being the respondent in the case, does not want to co-operate with the attempt at conciliation. Or, of course, friends or relatives may be bringing pressure to prevent his or her making an attempt at reconciliation. The order to attend makes it possible for the respondent to see the counsellor without appearing to make concessions, for he has no choice but to attend.

It would be too much to expect that many reconciliations attempted under subpoena are successful, but the court claims that the interviews often reduce the hostilities being waged between the partners, and this can result in a rather better future for the children. The division of property can sometimes be settled without recourse to the court, and on occasion a bitterly contested divorce action is avoided. The power to subpoena is extended to third parties, and from time to time it is used to enforce attendance of a mother-in-law or father-in-law. In such circumstances the consent of both husband and wife is first obtained to the issue of the subpoena. The court can also require, for instance, the woman with whom a husband is being unfaithful to attend the conciliation court. After her attendance, the court may order that she should not associate with the husband again.

It is now the normal practice in almost all parts of the world for marriage counselling to be undertaken on non-directive lines. How then does a counsellor attached to the Los Angeles conciliation court achieve this aim, representing as he does the legal authority? One counsellor's view is that the counsellor becomes 'a powerful authority figure in the eyes of the client, despite the fact that basically the counsellor is as non-authoritative as he would be in any setting'. It is difficult to see how a non-authoritarian role can really be achieved, even with the use of counsellors of considerable experience.

At the Los Angeles court the judge exercises direct control over all the work of the conciliation court, including the work of the counsellors. However, he does not do any counselling, as he has not been trained to do this; experience has shown, it is said, that an attempt by judges to engage in counselling has always ended in failure. Nevertheless, the judge has full access to the records of the reconciliation procedure, and if the husband and wife agreement is signed he sees the couple in his chambers, with the counsellor present, and congratulates them on the reconciliation. He also tells them that the court considers their marriage very important, and that it is in the society's interest that their marriage should be successful. This is thought to give couples the assurance of the court's support, and the feeling that the State has a direct interest in the maintenance of their marriage. The presiding judge has said that he 'has the duty to use every legal device, and the prestige of his position, to endeavour to save marriages rather than . . . perfunctorily pronounce "divorce granted" '.

The judge also takes a major part in the preliminary proceedings that take place before a divorce case comes up for hearing. He will normally see children in his chambers when questions of custody are involved, and asks them about their own feelings. This is apparently done informally, and the parties' lawyers are not present, although the judge usually discusses matters with the lawyers after he has seen the children. The court employs investigators to act on the court's behalf during custody proceedings. They act quite separately from the marriage counsellors, but their reports are made direct to the judge, who has control also of the conciliation work.

One of the greatest difficulties facing any reconciliation agency is the assessment of the effectiveness of its work. Perhaps the first of these difficulties is the problem of definition. What is 'success'? And how can it be measured in human terms? The Los Angeles conciliation court's answer to this question is reasonably simple: it follows up each and every reconciled case, one year after the reconciliation has taken place. The judge writes to the couple, enclosing a questionnaire which asks whether they are still living together as man and wife or, if not, when they separated. There is space for the couple to make their own comments, and they are sent a stamped envelope in which to return the questionnaire. The criterion for success is thus the state of the marriage one year after the original reconciliation took place. The court reports that a very high proportion of couples are in fact still living together after this period and that, measured by this standard, the effectiveness of its work has increased considerably in the past ten years.

Between 1954 and 1957, in cases where both husband and wife attended the court, an initial reconciliation rate of 43 per cent is reported. This figure rose in 1958 to 48 per cent, in 1959 to 49 per cent, in 1960 to 60 per cent and by 1963 stood at 64 per cent. These figures relate to those couples who appeared to be reconciled following the application to the court, and the follow-up research indicated that 75 per cent of these reconciled couples were still living together a year later. By this token, half the couples now coming before the conciliation court are sufficiently reconciled to be living together twelve months later. The court therefore claims that it is exercising a valuable social function, and it is now dealing with over 4,400 petitions a year.

The reconciliation ratio among couples who were already embarked on divorce proceedings when conciliation work started is rising steadily; it was reported as having risen from 30 per cent in 1955 to 55 per cent in 1960. It seems that the attention of many husbands and wives is drawn to the existence of the conciliation court through contacts with other branches of the legal system in Los Angeles. This may happen during the preliminary proceedings to the hearing of a divorce, such as applications for the custody of infant children, or for maintenance payments by the husband to the wife. It is perhaps for this reason that the court states that in over 90 per cent of the cases coming before it a divorce is neither necessary nor justified. Indeed, some reconciliations take place merely by reason of the fact that the petition has been filed, after letters confirming the first conference with a counsellor have been sent to the parties.

The beneficial effects of the reconciliation procedures of the Los Angeles court are claimed to extend beyond the improvement in the relationship between husband and wife. The court says it has noted a distinct improvement in its own relations with the public. It may also be that the concern evinced by the counsellors and by the judge helps the clients to feel that the operation of the law is humane and not impersonal.

The figures given earlier for the effectiveness of the conciliation procedures are, as the presiding judge points out, the product of a non-compulsory system used by a 'partially selective, reconciliation-prone group of couples'. In the first place, the very fact that one party to the divorce files a conciliation petition is a clear indication that he does not desire a quick divorce. The filing of the petition is not compulsory, and there is inevitably a built-in bias in favour of reconciliation, as must be the case for all voluntary marital reconciliation agencies. Secondly, referrals to the court are made by attorneys and by court officials who, having met one or both of the parties, feel that it would be worth while referring them to the conciliation court. Thirdly, only two-thirds of all divorce petitions filed in California are in fact followed in due course by a divorce decree. This contrasts with the figures for Great Britain, where about 90 per cent of all divorce petitions result in a divorce being ultimately granted. It seems that it is quite common for one partner, usually the wife, to file a divorce petition as a means of bringing pressure on her husband. If this pressure is successful, there is no longer any need for a divorce and the petition is withdrawn. This practice must clearly have an effect on the figures quoted. Another factor, claims the court, is that the skill and qualifications of its counsellors is reflected in the large number of successful reconciliations. Finally, the number of cases coming before the conciliation court is only one twenty-fifth of the number of divorce petitions filed in a year.

The cost of operating the conciliation court involves:

(a) employing qualified and trained marriage counsellors, each receiving a salary of approximately £4,700 a year

(b) employing a clerk to assist in the administrative work at the office of the court

(c) employing a shorthand typist

(d) provision of a counselling room, a waiting room and a clerk's office, with appropriate filing space.

One counsellor and the necessary supporting staff can deal with about seventy-five cases each month. In the Los Angeles court, cases are being dealt with at the rate of some 350 a month, and there are eleven counsellors on the staff.

During the year 1964-5, the cost of the salaries of individuals employed at the court was $180,748, i.e. approximately £75,300. These figures are made up as follows:

Supervising conciliation counsellor	$14,040
Other counsellors (eleven in all)	125,080
Clerks (seven in all)	33,720
Stenographer/secretary	7,908
	$180,748

On the basis that 4,400 petitions are now being dealt with

each year at the court, the cost of these salaries to the public purse is a little over $40 a case, or about £16 10s. This figure does not include the salary of the presiding judge, one of whose responsibilities is the supervision of the conciliation court, nor does it include the expense of maintaining and running the office. Nevertheless the court claims that the cost of running the service is small in relation to the results achieved. In 1963 the State of California spent $70,000,000 on giving aid to needy children, very many of whom came from broken homes. This is given as only one example of the weight of public expenditure that the court aims to reduce.

The court's clients come from all social scales and income groups; there are translation facilities for clients who cannot speak English. In fact, the husbands and wives who see the counsellors represent a fair cross-section of the community in that part of the United States. The great majority of the clients have children—over 88 per cent.

The presiding judge is not satisfied with the law relating to conciliation procedures in California, and for the future has suggested that there should be a substantial increase in the amount of research into the causes of marriage breakdown. He would also like to see provision for all counties in California to establish similar courts. This provision, he suggests, should include a financial levy on all divorce petitions filed in the courts. The filing fees would be increased and the money used to enable the work of the conciliation courts to be financed. He suggests that it should also be used to further the provision of pre-marriage education courses to be run in the local schools. 'No one,' the judge says, 'would think of eating peas off the back of his knife, or drinking coffee from a saucer, and we must instil a new code of social behaviour patterns relating to marriage which will promote and insure stability in American family life.'

The judge also suggests that the United States should amend its Constitution so that uniform requirements can be laid down for marriage and residential requirements, and also the grounds for divorce, throughout the country. Some States make a lot of money through the provision of easy divorces, and he considers that the work of the conciliation agencies must be adversely affected by the many different laws obtaining in the different States.

Other Conciliation Courts
California. Other conciliation courts in the State of California are operating at Sacramento, San Bernadino, San Luis Obispo, San Mateo, Alameda and Imperial County. Most of these courts were set up within the last few years, and with only minor variations they are organized on the same lines as the larger conciliation court in Los Angeles.

In Sacramento there is no attempt in the report of the court to claim percentage success in its work, although it has been found that, of those who were reconciled, 85 per cent were still living together a year after the 'reconciliation' took place. The court deals with over 600 cases a year, and has recently noted an increase in the number and rate of reconciliations. This court has under consideration a proposal that would make it obligatory for all couples starting divorce proceedings to have an interview with a marriage counsellor.

San Bernadino is distinguished by having a service for those clients who speak only Spanish, one of the clerks employed by the conciliation court acting as an interpreter. The court has been attached to the probation department and not to the superior court, and this has been felt to be a disadvantage. Attempts are also being made to improve the referral system to counselling agencies in the community, because clients have to go on a waiting list. One of these agencies, the Catholic Social Services, already receives referrals from the court and uses its own professional staff. Services are provided for all members of the community regardless of their religious belief, but the agency is not primarily concerned with marriage counselling. Nominal fees are charged by this agency.

In the county of San Bernadino there are almost as many divorces each year as there are marriages, the figures for 1964 being 3,765 divorces and 3,811 marriages. The conciliation court sees only about 350 cases each year; in these marriages about 750 children are involved.

At the San Luis Obispo court clients are invited to continue with counselling after a reconciliation has taken place. Only one counsellor is employed, however, and the court is in an area with a population of about 100,000 people. At San Mateo, over 400 cases come to the counsellors each year, and an average of three interviews is given in each case. More husbands file petitions than wives, and it is perhaps surprising that 10 per cent of all petitions are filed within the first year of marriage. Over 20 per cent of those people who file petitions have been married at least twice.

The conciliation court of San Diego handles over 1,250 cases a year, and uses three professional counsellors. This court has, and makes use of, the power to enforce attendance, but the service the court offers is essentially regarded as short-term counselling, as is the case with the Los Angeles court. The great majority of the 'reconciled' cases sign the husband and wife agreement, and do so after only one series of conferences, a series which involves one interview with each party and one joint interview. The danger of attempting to draw conclusions as to the success of this reconciliation work is clear from the fact that less than two-thirds of all divorce petitions in San Diego end with the grant of a decree. The figures for 1964 were 6,446 filings and 4,173 decrees of divorce. The difference between these figures clearly cannot be due solely to the operations of the conciliation court, which in the same period claimed only 232 reconciliations.

In the county of Alameda the divorce court has started to hold conferences in chambers with the parties and their lawyers. The judges are trying to cut through the strained reserve of the parties, which arises at least partly from the adversary proceedings, and to re-establish communication between them. If once this can be achieved the parties can be helped to tackle problems arising from the divorce proceedings. Lawyers in Alameda have co-operated with the court in holding these conferences, which sometimes result in a referral to the conciliation court, which is associated with the county probation department. In the first year of operations 530 couples came to the conciliation court, and a detailed assessment of this work has been made in the cases of sixty-nine of these couples who were regarded as having been successfully reconciled during the first six months. One year later sixty-six of these couples were traced, and it was found that forty-six were still living together, the remainder having separated or divorced. Further investigation showed that, of those who seemed to have been successfully reconciled, the majority were close to one another in age, belonged to the same social category, and had been married for five years or less. It also seemed that the chances of reconciliation seemed to increase with the number of children in the family.

In Imperial County there is one of the very few conciliation courts in California that offers long-term counselling. This is due to the fact that there are no counselling agencies in the community to which cases can be referred, and the court has no choice but to continue helping to the best of its ability. All couples with children under fifteen years of age are required to file a conciliation petition and to see a counsellor. In effect, this means that the counsellors are hard-pressed, and have to see as many as eight people in a day. The court considers that this impairs the effectiveness of the counsellor's work, and it is looking for more counsellors. There are presently only two counsellors available.

As in other parts of California, reluctant spouses can be compelled to appear at the Imperial County court, and the husband and wife agreement is used. This county was the second in the State of California to set up a conciliation court. Over a five-year period since the foundation of the court in 1959, 1,398 divorce actions were filed in Imperial County; in the same period 548 conciliation petitions were filed by those who had already filed for divorce. Reconciliations are claimed to have taken place in about 70 per cent of all cases, but this percentage is determined by considering only those couples who have two or more interviews. No one is required to have more than one interview. Perhaps a better means of assessing the service is that, of the 1,398 divorce petitions filed in the five-year period, 75 per cent ended in the grant of a decree. This is in fact a fairly high proportion when comparison is made with the national figures.

Contrary to the statements of other conciliation courts, the report of Imperial County indicates that the work initially meets with very little enthusiasm from lawyers. This may well be due to the additional work involved in the compulsory filing of a conciliation petition. When the court was first set up there was concern about the payment of the lawyers' fees, but it is the policy of the court, as in Los Angeles, to award reasonable fees to the attorney whether or not a reconciliation takes place. It has also been found that fees are paid more readily by reconciled couples than by those who remain apart.

Arizona. In Arizona, the first steps towards setting up conciliation machinery were taken in 1962, when the State Legislature permitted counties in the State to establish conciliation courts. In Maricopa County there is now a conciliation court which was formed after the judge in charge had visited other courts in the United States to observe the way in which they worked. The practice in the town of Phoenix, where the court is sited, is similar to the California courts. It is usual for one of the counsellors attached to the court to have a preliminary conference with the petitioner, then another with the respondent, and later a joint conference with them both. Third parties, including parents and others, can be called in for interview. No information from the counselling interviews appears on the court files. Before coming to see the counsellor, the parties make out a list of their complaints against one another, and are expected to mention such of their own characteristics as they feel may have contributed to the marriage difficulty. The counsellor sometimes administers a personality test as part of the counselling process.

It is found that lawyers refer nearly two-thirds of all the clients of the Maricopa county court, the remainder coming through friends, social agencies and as the result of newspaper articles. About 60 per cent of all petitions are by husbands and only 40 per cent by wives. In about half the cases there is already a divorce suit pending, so it would seem that a substantial number of husbands file conciliation petitions in order to counteract divorce proceedings commenced by their wives. The counsellors give an average of 3.6 interviews to each case, most of these interviews lasting an hour.

Montana. At Helena, in the State of Montana, a conciliation court similarly modelled on the Californian pattern is now operating, the expense of running it being shared between two adjoining counties. The only counsellor is operating the counselling service from her own home, which is not the practice in any other conciliation court. In the first two years of working in this way, just under 200 couples have been referred for counselling. It is claimed that 112 homes were 're-established' and that divorces were granted to only sixty-nine of the couples who were counselled.

Oregon. The circuit court of Portland, in the State of Oregon, has a conciliation division. A feature of the service provided by this division is that every effort is made to give immediate interviews to all who seek them, provided they live in the county. If potential clients live outside the county they are referred to other agencies such as the county mental health clinics, private psychiatrists and others. As every effort is made to see people without delay, the court sees its function as to deal with the crisis situation. Normally, clients are referred to other agencies if they need long-term help. The conciliation division compares itself to the emergency ward at a hospital, and when there is great pressure of work those people who seem to be immediately responsive to marriage counselling are given preference over those who seem likely to need more long-term help.

As with other conciliation courts there is power to subpoena the parties to attend for counselling, but only a few subpoenas have ever been issued. All counsellors have at least five years' counselling experience of the work before appointment. The previous requirement was ten years' experience of the work, but shortage of counsellors made it necessary to lower this standard. Counsellors' salaries rise from $8,064 a year on appointment to $9,744 after six years; the director of the division receives up to $11,256 a year.

An unusual provision is that all divorce petitioners are required to pay an additional fee, when commencing proceedings, towards the cost of maintaining the conciliation service. This is the only State in which a tax is levied on all divorces and used to subsidise a reconciliation service. The tax does not cover all the expenses of running the conciliation division of the Portland circuit court, and the balance is met by the county of Multnomah. Authority for this charge is contained in the statute which made it possible to set up conciliation courts in the State of Oregon.

The claims for the success of the work in this division are less than those made by many conciliation courts in other parts of the United States. Basing their figures on 531 cases seen in a recent year, the division states that 32 per cent became reconciled during a period of forty-five days from the commencement of proceedings. Some 40 per cent ended in divorce, and the remaining 28 per cent had neither divorced nor reconciled when the assessment was made.

The court procedures follow a regular pattern: a preliminary form has to be completed by the petitioner, and a conciliation petition filed. Letters offering appointments are termed by the court 'regular', 'friendly' or 'special'. The 'regular' letter reads as follows:

Dear Mrs Doe,

Your husband recently filed a Petition for Conciliation in this Court asking for a friendly confidential conference, as provided by law. He is being mailed a copy of this letter. Each of you is requested to be in the offices of the Conciliation Division, Court of Domestic Relations, located in the Multnomah County Court House, at .... on ....

A trained marriage counsellor will confer with both of you in private and will endeavor to assist you in resolving your marital difficulties.

Your husband is being sent a form similar to the enclosed one concerning the problems troubling your marriage. We invite you to do likewise with the enclosed form so that your Conciliation Counselor, who is impartial and equally interested in both of you, can understand both viewpoints. Please complete the enclosed form and bring it with you at the appointment time.

The time for your Conference has been reserved for you on our calendar. We trust you will keep this appointment voluntarily and avoid the necessity of requiring the Court to issue a subpoena. We will look forward to seeing you on the appointed day.

Very truly yours,

This letter is signed by the director of the conciliation division. The 'friendly' letter is shorter, and reads as follows:

Dear Mrs Doe,

We are writing to request that you come to our office for an interview on .... concerning your marital problems. This office is located at ....

Your husband will also be here for this interview and we

want you both to know that this conference is confidential, and that we are equally interested in each of your viewpoints.

Please complete the accompanying form and bring it with you to our office. Your husband has also been asked to complete a similar form.

Sincerely yours,

The form which the husband and wife are expected to complete and bring to the counsellor contains twenty-seven questions, ranging from the religious beliefs of the client to his or her wish for a reconciliation. Details are given of race, age, length of separation, schooling and employment. At the end of the form are more questions regarding the marriage difficulties. The form is headed 'This document is made secret by Law'.

A reconciliation order can be made by the judge, and a husband and wife agreement signed by both parties, similar to that in use in Los Angeles. If this happens they also receive a letter of congratulation signed by the judge. There is also an offer to give further help if this should become necessary.

Chapter 10

CANADA

In many respects the provision of marriage conciliation facilities in Canada is similar to that in the United States, although it would seem that developments have been less intensive. There are a few private practitioners offering marriage counselling for a fee, and several churches have pastoral counselling units which undertake marital work as part of the general service they offer. In family courts, an increasing number of which have been set up in Canada, counselling is given by trained and salaried probation officers attached to the courts. The most comprehensive conciliation service in the country is that operated by the various Family Service Associations, most of which are affiliated to the Family Service Association of America, which has its headquarters in New York.

This account will deal first with the operation of the family courts in different parts of Canada, and then go on to consider in detail the development of marriage conciliation work in Toronto, the second largest city in the country.

Family Courts

In six provinces of Canada, British Columbia, Alberta, Manitoba, Ontario, Quebec and Newfoundland, family courts have been set up, although in Quebec the court is called the social welfare court. Most of these family courts have resulted from an expansion of the work originally undertaken by the juvenile courts, and the duties and powers of the family courts vary slightly from province to province. The main purpose of the family court is to provide a social approach to family problems, the court using its officials, who are known as 'probation officers', to help with marital and other difficulties, provided the parties are willing to accept this help. There is no provision for any compulsory form of reconciliation in Canada, but in the social welfare courts in Quebec and in Newfoundland the judges are charged by law with the duty of acting as 'moderators' in any dispute between parents or between parents and children, where their services have been requested.[1]

In the other family courts in Canada, the judges are not given specific powers of mediation, and this work is left entirely to the probation officers, who are trained for it. The courts keep records of family problems and provide information and statistics on the incidence of these problems.

All the family courts co-operate with the other social service agencies, making referrals to them and accepting referrals from them, and some courts employ the services of a psychiatrist or make referrals to a psychiatric clinic. The court can make an order that people appearing before it should undergo diagnosis, or treatment, where this seems appropriate. It will be seen from this that there is inevitably some difficulty in defining the differing roles of the court, and in particular of the probation officers attached to the court. The court may have been approached for an order that will affect a marriage, and the probation officer may become responsible for seeing that the order, or some part of it, is carried out. At the same time the officer is expected to do what he can to see that the family problems are resolved and so becomes a conciliator. Probation officers are normally recruited from people who have had social work training, but it is often impossible for those who have come before the court to see the probation officer other than in an authoritarian role, in which case a referral may be made to a family service agency. It is recognized by the court that the service offered by the probation officers is in a different setting from that offered by the family service agencies, and that some people will be better suited to it than others. Some seem to benefit from the more authoritarian setting of the court while others can only accept help in a setting where they are free to come and go as they please.

At the present time the work of the family courts is confined to the making of orders that affect the various members of the family in relation to one another and in relation to the state, and does not extend to the grant of divorces. Those responsible for administering the courts feel that the problems of handling divorce cases would be too great for the family courts. This may possibly be an advantage, for those who come to a court which

[1] Courts of Justice Act (Revised Statutes, 1941, Chapter 15) 1950 The Family Courts Act, Chapter 118, R.S.N. 1952.

is known to be competent to grant divorces may find it difficult to accept from that same court a marital conciliation service.

As with all other courts offering marriage counselling and allied services, the records of the court are confidential. This is most important, for there are a large number of officials attached to the court. Apart from the judge and the probation staff there is the clerical staff and also, in the case of the larger courts, a psychiatrist or psychologist. In one family court, at Winnipeg, there is also an administrative officer who undertakes a good deal of the administrative work for the judge, and who supervises the probation officers. The term 'probation officer' may seem somewhat inappropriate for a worker who is doing marriage counselling, because of the inevitable association of his work with the supervision of people who have been found guilty of criminal offences. The title 'family counsellor' has been suggested as an alternative, but has not yet been adopted. However, it is probable that the clients who seek the officers' help do not feel much difficulty over the name. Those people who do will be more likely to go straight to the family service agency, or to some other source of help.

The family courts are not necessarily large: all that is strictly needed, apart from the courtroom, are small private offices for the use of the judge and the probation officer, and a general office for the clerical staff which also serves as a waiting room. Family courts are usually financed by the province, either alone or jointly with the municipal authorities. Those who work in the courts seem to prefer the arrangement where the province, the larger authority, pays for the cost of the courts. No doubt this is because there is less likelihood of the province having to reduce its expenditure from time to time because of financial stringency.

Most family courts are formed as a result of local pressure, usually an expression of public concern following an increase of marriage breakdown or juvenile delinquency. One such demand, framed in Edmonton in Alberta, stated that 'Jurisdictions over family matters and children in trouble are today scattered so that people are shunted from court to court with their problems. As a result it is impossible for the most well-meaning judge to make decisions based on the welfare of the whole family.'[1] This same demand said that the members of various professions, and of both government and private agencies, were tending to work against rather than in co-operation with each other. It was suggested that a family court could draw on the help of the counsellors working for private agencies, as well as those attached to the court itself.

Toronto

The first steps towards the establishment of marriage counselling services in Toronto took place in 1952, when the Canadian Mental Health Association and the Toronto Welfare Council held discussions on the need for such a service. A study committee was set up and representatives from the United States, including Dr David Mace, were invited to meet the committee and to address the various agencies in Toronto who were sponsoring the study of the need. In addition to the bodies already mentioned, these were the United Church of Canada and the Ontario Welfare Council. The National Marriage Guidance Council of the United Church of Canada, which in spite of its name is a very different organization from the National Marriage Guidance Council in Britain, made a formal request to the Toronto Welfare Council to consider what practical steps could be taken to improve co-operation between the professional agencies who were helping families that had got into difficulties, and to provide some form of training for those people who wanted to develop counselling skills. This led, in 1955, to a conference being held, at which time there were two different approaches being considered. The first approach, suggested by Dr Mace, was that a Marriage Guidance Council should be formed on similar lines to that operating in Britain, using carefully selected and trained volunteer workers supported by professionals. The alternative was the provision of services similar to those already operating in the United States.

Those who wanted to see a separate marriage counselling service, whether voluntary or paid, had argued that many people would not go to the family agencies for help because they were associated in the public mind with services given to people in a low social and economic category. On the other hand, those who were in favour of a development of the existing services said

[1] The Family Service Association of Edmonton, *Recommendations for Changes in Family Court Structure.* Edmonton 1965.

that a specialist marriage counselling service would be confusing to the general public. Accounts of work going on in the United States were given to the study committee, which ultimately recommended in favour of a very considerable strengthening of the then existing agencies, and although some members of the committee still thought that a separate marriage counselling agency should be provided, the majority opinion prevailed. The recommendations were made in 1957, and the present services operating in Toronto resulted from them.

Where counselling agencies in some countries depend largely or wholly on government money to carry on their work, the agencies in Toronto are primarily financed by the United Community Fund, a voluntary and charitable organization whose purpose is to act as a comprehensive agency for the collection and distribution of voluntarily donated money. The fund operates very much as would a commercial undertaking; it has the use of the services of an advertising agency, is run by prominent members of the community, and plans an annual campaign in considerable detail. The various organizations who receive money from the fund are required to refrain from making separate appeals for money, unless these have been agreed to in advance by the administrators of the fund.

Money is raised from individuals by way of annual subscription, and also from public functions, fashion shows and bazaars. Firms and business houses are also asked to contribute, as are charitable foundations. Other sources of income are bequests and legacies; these are sought by the fund, which advertises forms of legacy in its annual report. Over $9,000,000 is raised each year, of which less than 2 per cent goes on the administrative expenses of the fund. The remainder is distributed to various social agencies in the Greater Toronto area, and this includes those agencies that offer a marriage counselling service.

The Family Service Association of Metropolitan Toronto receives well over 90 per cent of its income from the fund, and the same is true of the North York and Weston Family Service Centre. The Catholic Family Services and the Jewish Family and Child Service also receive by far the greater part of their income from the fund, although they raise a higher proportion of their own funds than do the other services. The income of the fund is drawn from the following sources:

Firms and businesses	38·6%
Employees of firms	32·1%
Senior executive staff and the professions	19·7%
Private donors	8·5%
Students	1·1%

The fund-raising campaign is planned each year like a military operation. In May, each organization which receives money from the fund is expected to submit its budget for expenditure for the coming year. By this time the campaign committee has already started work and has estimated its ability to raise money in the months ahead. A target figure is then set by the committee, and during the summer months the campaign is carefully prepared. All agencies who hope to benefit from the success of the campaign are expected to take a part in it. The campaign itself is launched in October, and develops its full potential during the weeks preceding Christmas. After Christmas it is possible to begin to assess the results of the campaign, and during February the allocations of income for the year are made. By this time the whole process is about to recommence for the following year. The fund is administered by a board of trustees, who issue an annual report and accounts.

The primary service provided by the Family Service Association of Metropolitan Toronto is family counselling, which is described by the association as a skilled method of enabling individuals and families to develop more satisfying relationships by finding their own best ways of dealing with their problems. By far the greatest proportion of the cases handled by the association involve difficulties in marital relationships. The association uses over forty paid caseworkers, and its work has increased steadily in recent years. Most clients are referred to the association by other organizations, by their professional advisers or by their employers, but a very large number come on their own initiative.

As has already been noted, the major source of income of the association is the united community fund grant. Small sums are received by way of direct donations to the association and membership subscriptions, and clients pay a small fee for the services they receive. These fees range from $1 to $15 a week, and they are scaled according to the size and income of the family. There is no charge for the initial interview, and fees are waived for those who cannot afford to pay. The association receives only a little over 1 per cent of its income from the fees paid by clients.

The association works from seven district offices and two sub-centres, and its main offices are in the city of Toronto. In addition to the forty caseworkers there is an executive director, a director of casework, a psychiatric consultant and a director of public relations, as well as many other officers. A board of directors is generally responsible for the administration of the association. All caseworkers have to possess a Master of Social Work degree, which is awarded normally after two years' post-graduate training in social work. Caseworkers are recruited through advertising and through contacts that the association already has with students at the schools of social work. There are a great many contacts with doctors, lawyers and the other professions, particularly by way of referral to the association, but there is no formal relationship with any professional bodies.

Future plans for the association are at present limited because of a lack of funds and of trained staff. It can be clearly seen that the rate of expansion depends almost entirely on the support received from the union community fund, which in turn is dependent on the general public for support.

On the outskirts of Toronto are the districts of North York and Weston, where another family service centre operates. Like the Family Service Association of Metropolitan Toronto it receives almost all of its income (nearly 99 per cent) from the united community fund, and it spends the greater part of this income on salaries of its staff. It is also non-denominational, has no political affiliations and is privately organized. A community of over 350,000 is served, and it is estimated that over 47 per cent of the new cases involve the caseworkers in marriage coun-selling. Some of the work is done in groups, but most counselling goes on in personal interviews between the client and the indivi-dual caseworker. All appointments for interviews, whether at the main centre or at the branch office, are made by the recep-tionist at the main centre.

The family service centre charged fees on a sliding scale according to the income of the clients between the years 1961 and 1965, but since then there has been no specified charge.

Instead, the client is given the responsibility of deciding the amount of the fee that he can pay. He fills this amount in on a form when he first comes for interview, and usually pays the fee at the same time as the interview. In the first six months of operation of the new scheme, as much money was collected from clients as in the previous period of twelve months. Over half the clients of the centre paid no fee at all, and some receive financial help from the centre. The form on which the client is asked to indicate the amount he can pay contains the following:

'The agency's primary concern is to serve people in the best possible way, and we do not want to burden you with obligations which would be hard to meet. You are the best judge of your own financial commitments. Therefore, we ask you to indicate on the scale below the amount you think you can afford to pay *for each interview*, with due regard for your income and financial commitments. The fee you indicate will cover each interview, regardless of how many of your family members are participating. Please circle the amount you want to pay for each interview:

$ 0 1 2 3 4 5 6 7 8 9 10 11 12 13 14 15 16 17 18 19 20

If your financial circumstances change, you may ask to have your fee adjusted accordingly.'

Group counselling is offered to fifty or more couples at any given time, and the centre finds that this type of counselling has enabled them to increase considerably the number of people who have been helped. The centre believes that group counselling is in fact a more effective method of helping many couples than individual counselling. The method demands specially trained counsellors, and only a few of the staff are so trained. There are more potential clients for these groups than can be accommodated by the centre at the present time.

Pressures of a financial and personal nature have led the centre to the conclusion that the only answer to its problems is to seek financial aid from the government by way of subsidy, or possibly by the government taking over the role of the private agency. Short of additional help of this kind the centre has two alternatives. The first is to reduce the standard of the work done so that only an emergency service is offered; the second is to maintain the present standards while turning away an ever-increasing number of clients. Steps are already being considered whereby the centre may be linked more formally to the Family Service Association, and a standing committee has recently been set up to study ways in which additional volunteer help can be used.

The other organizations in Toronto who are providing marriage counselling are doing so under the auspices of the churches. There are the Catholic Family Services, the Toronto Institute of Family Relations (sponsored by the United Church of Canada) and the Jewish Family and Child Service. Both the Catholic and the Jewish Services receive more than half their income from the United Community Fund, but a large proportion also comes from members of their own faiths. The majority of clients of these services come from the labouring classes; the Jewish service reports that about two-thirds of their clients come into this category, and that only 5.1% are from the professional classes.

The Toronto Institute of Family Relations offers a pastoral counselling service, and uses ordained clergymen who have had special training in social work. There are many similar services operating in Canada; they do not normally charge fees, and they are financed by the churches to which they are attached. Clients do not have to be members of the same church as the counsellors, who make referrals to other agencies where this seems appropriate. It is quite normal for a local pastoral counselling service to consist of one counsellor supported by a part-time secretary and by a part-time psychiatric consultant. There may be as many as twenty or more counselling hours given each week by the counsellor at such an agency, and both individual and group counselling methods are in use.

It will be seen that pressures of time, finance and staff shortage are causing considerable difficulty for the existing agencies in Canada, and that some of them are thinking in terms of seeking state aid, and of enlisting suitable voluntary help to support the work being done by the professional caseworkers. Family courts are operating an official service which includes marriage conciliation work, and which is very closely linked to the other functions of the courts, but most people who seek marriage counselling do so from the private agencies.

COMMENTARY

It is difficult to form an adequate impression of a rapidly developing organization. This difficulty is multiplied many times when one is trying to assess a series of different developments, as is the case in the present study of marital conciliation systems. There are many experiments going on in this field and, as has been noted in the previous chapters, organizations in different countries have tackled the problem in different ways. It is nevertheless easy to discern a quickening interest in the provision of marriage conciliation by one means or another, it being understood in all parts of the world that society has a vested interest in the preservation of the family as a unit.

From experience in many quarters it seems clear to me that any attempt to provide marital conciliation under duress is doomed to failure from the outset. Unless one, or preferably both, of the parties have at least some motive for preserving the marriage, nothing is to be gained from applying a process of law that forces them to try to make up their differences. I do not mean to imply by this that the provision of conciliation services in association with the courts of law is inappropriate. Far from it. Nevertheless, I suggest that it is only when the parties take advantage of these services on a voluntary basis that there is any likelihood of their being given effective help.

It seems to be clearly established that, even when a marriage has irretrievably broken down, there is a very real case for providing counselling facilities for both husband and wife. A service of this kind enables them to consider the practical and the emotional problems that are going to result from their divorce, and will often reduce the serious effects that breakdown will have on any children of the marriage. Furthermore, much judicial time can be saved if husbands and wives can settle between them some of the practical results of the ending of their marriage. Property disputes are less likely, maintenance claims and demands for the custody of children will come less frequently before the courts, if the parties receive appropriate help in good time.

Those concerned with the provision of marriage counselling services with the use of selected and trained voluntary workers are often asked whether these workers have either the experience or the training to give adequate help to people with marital problems. Suggestions are made from time to time that the voluntary worker is more likely to do harm than good, and that all marriage counselling work should be done by people who have had a considerable amount of training, and who work on a professional basis. My own view is that the firmly established services in Great Britain, Australia and New Zealand, all of which are now dealing with many thousands of cases every year, have proved beyond all doubt that the volunteer can be of great value, subject to certain important safeguards. In the first place it is generally accepted that a rigorous and searching process of selection is essential; secondly, an adequate form of basic training or orientation is required; and thirdly, that continuous in-service training in the form of professional supervision and case discussion is absolutely necessary. Volunteer counsellors have to be trained to understand the limits of their own competence, and supervised to ensure that they stay within those limits. Supervision has the additional advantage of enabling counsellors to make a steady improvement in the skills of their work. It seems to me that the procedure in New Zealand, under which counsellors are required to work regularly and under which they receive close supervision, especially if they have stopped work for even a limited time, is the best that has so far been devised.

It is normally too late to be able to give much help in saving a marriage by the time the parties have reached the divorce court. To my mind it is essential for those countries who have adopted a divorce law to make adequate provision at the same time for a service of marriage conciliation. It does not seem to me to be particularly significant whether this service is provided by the government or by private individuals or organizations, as long as it is available. The important thing is that it should be provided, and that the counsellors should be properly selected, trained and supervised. The system in Britain, under which the service operates under the control of a voluntary organization which receives financial support from the government, has been found to work well. At the same time, the operation of private organizations using paid workers and supported by Community Funds, as in the United States and in Canada, has also been shown to be effective.

Not only is it essential that a marriage counselling service should be provided. It is also vitally important that people in the community should know that it exists and that they should be given every opportunity, at the earliest stage, to seek counselling help on an entirely voluntary basis.

INDEX

For Product Safety Concerns and Information please contact our EU
representative GPSR@taylorandfrancis.com
Taylor & Francis Verlag GmbH, Kaufingerstraße 24, 80331 München, Germany

www.ingramcontent.com/pod-product-compliance
Lightning Source LLC
Chambersburg PA
CBHW050445280326
41932CB00013BA/2245